TO KNOW HIM, TO LOVE HIM, TO SERVE HIM

forming Parish Evangelisation Teams

Paul Cannon & Sharon Beech

CONTENTS

BIOGRAPHIES

Fr Paul Cannon was ordained priest for the Diocese of Salford in 1982. In 1987 he was appointed as a team member at the Catholic Missionary Society, based in London. From 1991 to 1994 he served as Director of the Catholic Missionary Society. On completion of his term of office at the CMS he studied for his masters degree in Adult Religious Education at Loyola University, Chicago. He is currently the parish priest of Our Lady of Good Counsel and Guardian Angels in Bury, Lancs. His experience at the CMS and experience of working in the field of evangelisation has meant that together with Sharon Beech he has been called upon by dioceses to help them to form Missionary Teams. In 2014, along with Sharon Beech, he was commissioned by Redemptorist Publications to write ***Welcome to Witness: Becoming an evangelising parish.*** Over the years he has been a regular contributor to Redemptorist Publications' Sunday Plus weekly bulletin, particularly on evangelisation and formation through the medium of film.

Sharon Beech is a mother of three and has five grandchildren and has worked for Salford Diocese for twenty-one years. She is the Pastoral and Administrative Assistant at the Church of Our Lady of Good Counsel and Guardian Angels in Bury, Lancashire. She has a bachelors and masters degree in Theology and Religious Studies and has written on the *impact of Christianity on the Inuit* and the *anthropology of ritual in a secular society*. She has been involved in the work of evangelisation for many years and jointly with Fr Paul has been called upon to work with several dioceses throughout England and Wales in presenting programmes to help them form missionary parishes. In the past she has written for the Paulist evangelisation ministries in Washington DC and was co-author with Fr Paul Cannon of ***Welcome to Witness: Becoming an evangelising parish.***

INTRODUCTION

In his homily on Sunday 25 September 2016, during the Jubilee of Mercy Mass for Catechists, Pope Francis stressed that God is shared with the world through love and authentic relationships, not by forcing the truth on people. He said:

We are called always to live out and proclaim the newness of the Lord's love: "Jesus truly loves you, just as you are. Give him space: in spite of the disappointments and wounds in your life, give him the chance to love you. He will not disappoint you".

It is by loving that the God-who-is-Love is proclaimed to the world: not by the power of convincing, never by imposing the truth, no less by growing fixated on some religious or moral obligation. God is proclaimed through the encounter between persons, with care for their history and their journey. Because the Lord is not an idea, but a living person: his message is passed on through simple and authentic testimony, by listening and welcoming, with joy which radiates outward. We do not speak convincingly about Jesus when we are sad; nor do we transmit God's beauty merely with beautiful homilies. The God of hope is proclaimed by living out the Gospel of love in the present moment, without being afraid of testifying to it, even in new ways.

Through this book we hope that parishes will feel encouraged to look afresh at the endless possibilities and opportunities of reaching out to people in love, sharing their community's faith and the individual faith of members of the parish with each other and with those who feel that they are outside of the Church, or that they may not be welcomed by the Church.

Evangelisation is the central mission of the Church's activity. All of us from time to time need to take stock of our faith-life and our commitment to fulfilling our basic Christian duty, bestowed upon us in our baptism: going out to the whole world proclaiming Jesus Christ.

The starting point for us all must be an evaluation of our personal relationship with Jesus Christ, for we have been called into that relationship by Christ himself.

We hope that this book will encourage parishes to form a Parish Evangelisation Team, not solely as the ones "doing" the work of evangelisation, but a team encouraging all members of the parish to see the opportunities presented to them to evangelise in their everyday life and through the life of the parish community. We feel that parishes need a team of people, who have prayed together and been formed as a team through reflection, to lead the way in assessing where the parish currently is in relation to evangelising, and who will look at new methods and practices which will encourage people to discover the call to be disciples in the world.

In his book, *Divine Renovation: From a Maintenance to a Missional Parish* (Toronto: Novalis, 2014), Fr James Mallon reflected on the tragic event of the sinking of the **RMS Titanic**. He said that he realised that there could be a metaphor for the Church in this story. He referred to the way in which only two of the eighteen lifeboats from the *Titanic* went to rescue survivors in the freezing waters of the North Atlantic Ocean. The other sixteen sat a safe distance away from where the ship sank and where the survivors in the freezing waters were. He says that he was struck by the fact that we (the Church) exist for mission and that, like Jesus, we have been sent to "seek and save" and yet so often as a Church we sit at a safe distance, more concerned with our own needs and comfort.

The creation of Parish Evangelisation Teams can help us to be more like the lifeboats that do what they are designed to do: go and save people. The creation of a team of people focused on evangelisation will naturally create a new focus in the parish, where, if we are rather inward-looking, we will change and open the doors to go out and celebrate and share our faith in our neighbourhood, in our homes and our workplaces.

In the formation meetings we have focused on why we evangelise, through the use of Pope Paul VI's *Evangelii Nuntiandi.* Then using some of Pope Francis' words and ideas from *Evangelii Gaudium, Laudato Si'* and *Amoris Laetitia,* we have tried to widen the focus of evangelisation from simply looking at what happens in our own parish, to how we can reach out to many more people. Each meeting has prayer, scripture, reflection and discussion and our hope is that the time of formation leads to a new prayerful and reflective evangelising conscience in our parishes.

CHAPTER ONE

Why form a Parish Evangelisation Team?

The answer to the question "Why form a Parish Evangelisation Team?" would appear to be quite simple. If we follow the example of Jesus and listen to his call, then we simply must entrust his work to those who will ensure it is fulfilled in our parishes and in our lives.

In July 2015 we were fortunate to be involved at grass-roots level with the organisation of the first National Conference on Evangelisation, *Proclaim 15*, which was held in Birmingham and hosted over 1000 people from England and Wales who either work, or are in involved in the work of evangelisation in our parishes. We were happy to accept the invitation of the Catholic Bishops' Conference of England and Wales to present a workshop on Parish Evangelisation Teams. Imagine our surprise when Cardinal Nichols, Archbishop Longley of the Archdiocese of Birmingham and Bishop Nicholas Hudson, the bishop with responsibility for the conference, were to focus their keynote speeches and press releases prior to the start of the conference around the importance of Parish Evangelisation Teams. No pressure there, then?

"I invite all Christians everywhere at this very moment to a renewed personal encounter with Jesus Christ or at least an openness to letting him encounter them"
– Pope Francis, Evangelii Gaudium

Just as Jesus chose twelve trusted men to work alongside him and to teach and carry his word forward, so too we as a Church, and in particular our parishes, need to gather together a group of people to help the parish focus on the centrality of the Word of God and the work of **evangelisation.**

We are all members of the Church today, not simply through an accident of birth – which means that by being baptised into the Church we are called to follow Jesus – but because Jesus himself called us and in doing this he was carrying out the will of the Father in calling each one of us to follow him in his mission.

On the 27 February 2015 in his first Lent homily Fr Raniero Cantalamessa, the preacher to the Pontifical Household, reported that:

Written at the end of the Synod of Bishops on the New Evangelisation, the Exhortation [*Evangelii Gaudium*] presents three poles of interest, which are intertwined: the subject, the object and the method of the evangelisation: who must evangelise, what must be evangelised, how should one evangelise. In regard to the evangelising subject the Pope says that it is constituted by all the baptised:

"In virtue of their baptism, all the members of the People of God have become missionary disciples (cf. Matthew 28:19). All the baptised, whatever their position in the Church or their level of instruction in the faith, are agents of evangelisation, and it would be insufficient to envisage a plan of evangelisation to be carried out by professionals, while the rest of the faithful would simply be passive recipients. The new evangelisation calls for personal involvement on the part of each of the baptised." **(EG 120)**

At the ***Proclaim 15*** National Evangelisation Conference in Birmingham, 11 July 2015, Cardinal Nichols said:

We are here because it is the will of the Father to send us into the world!

Think of the calling of the first twelve disciples, the apostles. No one forced them to follow. They were invited. They were called to be with Jesus. That was the first step: called into a communion of life with him, into a "divine *communio*".

They were so different. Just think of this. Matthew was a tax collector, hated by most people as a traitor, a collaborator with the oppressive Roman authorities. Simon was a Zealot, committed to the liberation of his people. They were called together by Jesus. In any other circumstance, Simon would have knifed

Matthew, killing him on the spot. In the *communio* of Jesus something else is at work, something which is far greater than human commitment, a human cause.

Despite an apparent decline in the church-going population there is an unprecedented movement towards the work of the Spirit. This is because the model of Church is changing and Pope Francis has injected a new hope and vision into the Church. The Church has a new energy and parishes are talking about **evangelisation**: that word which was completely alien in a Catholic environment is now the buzzword for the future. Each parish has its own unique family of faith, its own dynamic, drawn from its demographic and cultural structure, this determines the way in which its community sustains its faith-life within a given area. No longer do dogma and doctrine alone sustain a parish community and, although these don't change, the challenge is to send out the message of Jesus Christ as one of love and hope for all people whatever their situation.

It is this message that is at the very core of the "why" of forming Parish Evangelisation Teams. Within this work, the Holy Spirit provides all the gifts necessary to create and fulfil a healthy vision of Church. These gifts are sufficient to do this work and just as Jesus promised, we have not been left orphans. He is with us always!

In line with Canon Law, parishes are required to have a Pastoral Council or a Finance Council. However, it is surprising that there is no mention in the Code of Canon Law of a requirement for a parish to have a specific group of people who are responsible for evangelisation in a parish. Does it seem strange that the one mandate passed down from Jesus as the central mission of the Church is not a requirement in Canon Law?

Perhaps one reason for its absence from Canon Law is that to give such a group in a parish canonical status could, in fact, cause some problems. As we explore the possibilities of establishing and forming a Parish Evangelisation Team we will see that there is a downside and upside to establishing such a team.

The Year of Faith (2012–2013), called by Pope Emeritus Benedict XVI and ending during the pontificate of Pope Francis, provided the Church with a valuable opportunity for the people in our parishes to reflect on their faith, to grow in faith and perhaps feel more confident to share their faith with others.

In 2013 Pope Francis gave us possibly the most important but certainly the most innovative and definitive exhortation on evangelisation, *Evangelii Gaudium* ("The Joy of the Gospel"). With this document he has thrown down a gauntlet to the whole Catholic Church and its people when he says:

I invite all Christians, everywhere, at this very moment, to a renewed personal encounter with Jesus Christ, or at least an openness to letting him encounter them; I ask all of you to do this unfailingly each day. No one should think that his invitation is not meant for him or her, "since no one is excluded from the joy brought by the Lord". The Lord does not disappoint those who take this risk; whenever we take a step towards Jesus, we come to realise that he is already there waiting for us with open arms. (EG 3)

A personal story – Denis' story

Someone who was thinking of becoming a Catholic in our parish, a gentleman named Denis who has sadly since died, asked us, "What is evangelisation?" We gave what we thought was a succinct answer: "Proclaiming the Gospel message to other people through word and action." The response, however, came as a complete surprise: "Really? Do you mean Catholics do that?"

We certainly do. In fact, this is central to our identity and mission as a Church. Without sharing the Gospel message, the Church will die. The word "evangelisation" has often been spoken about in theory and we have shied away from its practical application. But times are changing. The Year of Faith which ended in 2013 began with the 2012 Synod of Bishops on the New Evangelisation (and they did not try to use another word!). In 2015 Pope Francis called for a Jubilee Year of Mercy, once again highlighting the need for us to reach out to those of our brothers and sisters who are in need

and to proclaim God's abiding mercy and love. We must then reach out to people who are or were part of the Church and need help to reawaken their faith. We must also turn to those searching for new meaning in their lives. St John Paul II first coined the phrase "the New Evangelisation"; Pope Benedict called a Synod on that same theme and created the Pontifical Council for the Promotion of the New Evangelisation; Pope Francis is encouraging all of us to "go out and do it".

Parish Evangelisation Teams

It is very difficult to explain fully what a Parish Evangelisation Team is. This is because there are mixed ideas about it and there is a real danger that Parish Evangelisation Teams may feel that they are the only ones who are to evangelise, and some will not be able to resist the temptation of doorstep evangelising (as referred to by Cardinal Nichols at *Proclaim 15*). So here is a phrase that we must make a mantra for this book and for the time of formation: **Parish Evangelisation Teams are the evangelising conscience of the parish.**

In taking on this mission, Parish Evangelisation Teams are called to enrich and enhance the work and the life of the parish, ensuring that the parish is open to the workings of the Holy Spirit in every situation. In forming Parish Evangelisation Teams each parish enables its congregation to have the tools to follow Jesus, to reach out to those struggling to find Jesus' meaning for them and to put his hope for us at the centre of our lives. Every parish is a family of believers and in his apostolic exhortation, *Amoris Laetitia*, Pope Francis says:

This Exhortation is especially timely in this Jubilee Year of Mercy. First, because it represents an invitation to Christian families to value the gifts of marriage and the family, and to persevere in a love strengthened by virtues of generosity, commitment, fidelity and patience. Second, because it seeks to encourage everyone to be a sign of mercy and closeness wherever family life remains imperfect or lacks peace and joy. **(AL 5)**

This is why we need to set up Parish Evangelisation Teams.

But how do we do "it"?

By becoming a parish that evangelises by **witness** and **proclamation**.

CHAPTER TWO

How to set up a Parish Evangelisation Team

From why to how

From a practical point of view if we are asked the question "Why?" we should be prepared to answer the subsequent question "How?" This chapter will provide a practical approach to setting up Parish Evangelisation Teams. Of course, who better to help us focus on the task ahead than Pope Francis?

Pope Francis describes the parish in "The Face of Mercy" (*Misericordiae Vultus*) as, "Wherever there are Christians everyone should find an oasis of mercy" (MV 12), and in *Evangelii Gaudium* he describes it as a "sanctuary where the thirsty come to drink in the midst of their journey a community with an endless desire to show mercy" (EG 28).

The task of forming a Parish Evangelisation Team will initially fall to the parish clergy and the guidelines that follow are designed as just that – guidelines. In embracing this task, the parish will be called to rethink and review what, for some, has become the status quo. As Pope Francis says regarding becoming a truly evangelising parish:

I dream of a "missionary option", that is, a missionary impulse capable of transforming everything… so that the [parish's] customs, ways of doing things, times and schedules, language and structures can be suitably channelled for the evangelisation of today's world rather than for her self-preservation. (EG 27)

Setting up a Parish Evangelisation Team

Our advice to parish clergy, in the first instance, is not just to invite the usual suspects, who are probably heavily involved in the life of the parish already, but to seek out some new people who they feel could work in a team, has shown an interest in evangelisation, who would understand that it was not their job to do all the evangelisation work in the parish, but to ensure that the parish put evangelisation into all areas of parish life. Cast your nets widely for potential team members. Don't just go to the people who are already doing a lot, but make a broad appeal. Invite people personally and through the parish newsletter.

When setting up the team it is advisable to explain to the group that the project would be self-generating and would not place a lot more work on their shoulders but would also mean that the parishioners would be taking a more active part in the central mission of the Church's evangelisation.

- Invite 8–10 people from the parish (who have either expressed an interest in evangelisation or who you feel would make good members of the Parish Evangelisation Team) to come together and meet with the parish clergy
- At the introductory meeting, outline the programme of formation for the team (all the programme contained within this book), which will involve reflection on the Church in the modern world and evangelisation
- The team can then begin to meet together in a time of formation and prayer
- At the end of the time of formation the parish priest could, if he feels it is appropriate, commission the Parish Evangelisation team in the presence of the parish community on a given Sunday. In commissioning the team, the parish priest will have an opportunity to explain what exactly their role is, their responsibilities to the whole parish and how others will be drawn into this vital ministry
- After the commissioning, the Parish Evangelisation Team will need to be supported in their ministry by the parish clergy. The team will need to constantly engage in the work of finding new resources for themselves and the people in the parish.

The downside for Parish Evangelisation Teams can be that if they do not undergo a time of formation and reflection they may feel that they are the only ones in the parish who have to do all the evangelising (the danger of giving them canonical status as mentioned before). They can also easily burn out if they have unreal expectations of themselves (or if others have unreal expectations of the team). Any evangelisation work will fail without prayerful reflection and openness to the guidance of the Holy Spirit.

The upside of the existence of a Parish Evangelisation Team in a parish is that with a good perspective, good formation and patience, they can help a parish community (and the individuals in the community) to adapt its thinking, so that more parishioners see how they are firstly called to be evangelisers, and secondly, how they can become involved in evangelisation. The team can help a parish to see more clearly how most parish programmes and parish events are opportunities for evangelisation, and they can play their part in helping their parish to move from being a good welcoming parish to an excellent inviting parish.

The Parish Evangelisation Team

Who should you consider inviting to be on the team?

- Committed Catholics
- People who are open to new ways of doing things
- Ideally some people who have experience with the unchurched or the lapsed

- People who are able to work with people who have doubts
- People who are non-judgemental and flexible
- People who are not overly committed already
- A group of people who are a good mixture of age ranges and male and female.

How to select the people to invite to be part of the team

- Invite people personally, as well as inviting people through the newsletter to indicate their interest (stressing that not everyone will be able to be a part of the team but there will be plenty of work in the area of evangelisation once the team has been formed)
- Try not to ask those who are already over-burdened or over-involved in ministry
- Seek out those who you feel are open to new experiences of God through others
- Seek out those who you feel are going to be good at working as part of a team
- Seek out those who have shown an interest, for example, in *Evangelii Gaudium*, especially as this is going to be the blueprint for mission and evangelisation for many years to come.

What will they do during the time of formation?

This will be the time when they will be invited to become familiar with some of the basic Church texts related to evangelisation, especially in the context of the parish. Over a series of meetings, they will have the opportunity to look at the Gospel mandate

for mission and its implications and then to move forward to some of the key ideas from Paul VI's encyclical, *Evangelii Nuntiandi* (1975), leading to a fuller appreciation of Pope Francis' *Evangelii Gaudium, Laudato Si'* and *Amoris Laetitia.*

After the time of formation, they will explore a simple review of the parish as it is now in terms of evangelisation, looking at:
- Where the parish is now
- What needs to change
- What can be improved
- What the parish's strengths and weaknesses are
- Evaluating how evangelisation is seen in the parish
- Who or which groups are actively and consciously involved in evangelisation at the moment.

They will finish their time of formation reflecting on what it means to be Church in a secular society.

The purpose of the time of formation is:

- Firstly, to form a group of people into a team who can work together and draw on their different strengths, skills and talents
- To form a team who have a basic understanding of the call to evangelisation and its priority in the life of the Church
- To begin the process of identifying the work that lies ahead in making the whole parish community more missionary and evangelisation-minded
- To begin to identify what is already happening and promote new opportunities and methods of being an evangelising (and inviting) parish.

Important principles for the Parish Evangelisation Team

- They must pace themselves – not try to run before they have learned to walk and be careful of burnout through trying to do too much too quickly
- Resist the temptation to just get on with it without using the time of formation and the time for prayerful preparation
- They must be realistic in setting their goals at the end of the formation period (remember it is God's Church and we are merely servants of the Church)
- They must learn to utilise, encourage and resource existing groups, ministries and individuals
- They must remain connected to, and in communication with, the parish clergy and the whole parish community
- Finally, it is hoped, they will eventually see that they are to be in a very gentle way **the evangelising conscience of the parish**, constantly asking the question about all parish activity: How does this relate to evangelisation? This will lead to a new way of being a parish and most likely a new way of using our parish resources.

In all of this the team must be open to the workings of the Holy Spirit. Sometimes the Holy Spirit has a different take on what we think was a wonderful plan, so always be open to the guiding hand of the Spirit.

Review and plan

After completing the time of formation the Team can meet to review its mission, making a list of strengths and weaknesses which can form the basis of a plan for the team.

The team can begin to explore a simple review/audit of the parish as it is now in terms of evangelisation (*see* Chapter Seven for the **parish audit** and **action plan**), looking, as we said above, at where the parish is now, what needs to change, what can be improved, what the parish's strengths and weaknesses are, and evaluating how evangelisation is seen in the parish and who or which groups are actively and consciously involved in evangelisation at the moment. This exercise can inform the creation of a plan of action for evangelisation.

"Our generation is invited to generously reach out to others in our communities"

Paul Cannon & Sharon Beech, Welcome to Witness

And now a final thought to emphasise the urgency of this task…

In a recent survey, British Social Attitudes 28 (London: National Centre for Social Research, 2012) we find:

- Half (50 per cent) of the participants do not regard themselves as belonging to a particular religion
- 65 per cent of 18–24-year-olds do not affiliate to a religion compared with 55 per cent of the same age group (18–27) in 1983
- Around one in ten are Roman Catholic
- Overall 79 per cent of the British public describe themselves as having been brought up in a particular religion
- 56 per cent of those affiliating to a religion or brought up in a religion never attend religious services or meetings

- 29 per cent of Catholics never attend church; 20 per cent of Catholics attend church once a year
- Quote: "On the basis of our findings it seems likely that the **ongoing decline in religious affiliation** (and consequently religious attendance) will continue. This reflects the fact that each generation is less likely than its predecessor to be born into religious families and that this lack of religiosity tends to remain with an individual as they get older."

There is our challenge: **It doesn't have to be this way.** Our generation is invited to respond to this situation, to generously reach out to others in our communities. But we can't do it alone. We need to have Parish Evangelisation Teams.

CHAPTER THREE

Reflecting on *Evangelii Nuntiandi*

Formation Meetings 1 and 2

Introduction to Meetings 1 and 2 – *Evangelii Nuntiandi*

(to be read before the meetings)

The work of evangelising is not a task to be fulfilled only by the ordained. In the past it was predominantly the work of the priest and religious, either at home or overseas. However, the primary role of the priest is to **equip the saints for the work of ministry,** as St Paul says in his letter to the Ephesians (4:12-16). A priest in a parish cannot carry out the mission of the Church in that particular location in isolation. Some try, but they usually end up suffering from burnout, or give up out of frustration! In "What is the New Evangelisation? Why is it important for priestly formation?" Ralph Martin, reflecting on *Evangelii Gaudium*, says that the "'new evangelisation' must involve an awakening to a deeper understanding of the role of priestly leadership in equipping and empowering lay holiness and mission"; (<https://www.renewalministries.net/files/freeliterature/what_is_the_newevangelization_ipf_symposium_2010_407_10.pdf>, accessed 7 Oct. 2016).

During this time of formation, we feel it is important that the team appreciate the fundamental role that successive popes have taken in the promotion of evangelisation and how they have strived to focus the faithful on their unique role in the work of evangelisation.

Coming on the heels of Vatican II, the 1974 Synod of Bishops were to find the definition of evangelisation somewhat problematic and therefore it fell to Pope Paul VI to draw together the document that would set the Catholic world on its head.

> *"The whole Church is therefore called upon to evangelise, and yet within her we have different evangelising tasks to accomplish"*
>
> – Pope Paul VI, Evangelii Nuntiandi

Over the years we had come to expect that papal encyclicals and apostolic exhortations were written for the magisterium and a small number of people who understood their relevance. *Evangelii Nuntiandi* ("On Evangelisation in the Modern World") was written in 1975, close to the end of the fifteenth year of the pontificate of Pope Paul VI, and it was to become the most important apostolic exhortation of its time. This document was directed at Christians everywhere and reaffirmed the need to spread the Gospel to all nations. It was also the first document to come out of a General Synod of Bishops.

Many experts in the field of evangelisation agree that this is the greatest pastoral document that has ever been written. Pope John Paul II was to make frequent reference to its content in *Gaudium et Spes,* quoting:

Man, who is the only creature on earth which God willed for itself, cannot fully find himself except through a sincere gift of himself. (GS 24)

Similarly, Pope Francis makes frequent reference to *Evangelii Nuntiandi* in his exhortation *Evangelii Gaudium*, saying the words of *Evangelii Nuntiandi* "are as timely as if they had been written yesterday and furthermore to my mind the greatest pastoral document that has ever been written to this day" ("The Best Books I Read in 2013", <www.catholicworldreport.com, 1 January 2014>, accessed 7 Oct. 2016).

Therefore, we feel that this is the appropriate place to begin the time of formation with some reflection on *Evangelii Nuntiandi*. Pope Paul VI speaking in *Evangelii Nuntiandi* says both the conversion of consciences and conversion of culture are necessary and makes the point that verbal proclamation is incomplete without the witness of life, but that witness of life is also incomplete without the proclamation of "the name, the teaching, the life, the promise, the kingdom and the mystery of Jesus of Nazareth, the Son of God" (EN 22). In other words, for the first time we are being told that it's not just enough to talk about conversion but that in proclaiming that Jesus is our Saviour we need to witness to it in our lives and in how we live our lives. Furthermore, it is our mission to make it happen.

The witness that the Lord gives of Himself and that Saint Luke gathered together in his Gospel – "I must proclaim the Good News of the kingdom of God" (Luke 4:43) – without doubt has enormous consequences for it sums up the whole mission of Jesus: "That is what I was sent to do" (Luke 4:43). These words take on their full significance if one links them with the previous verses, in which Christ has just applied to Himself the words of the prophet (Isaiah 61:1) "The Spirit of the Lord has been given to me for he has anointed me. He has sent me to bring the good news to the poor." (EN 6)

In asking us to witness to ourselves and our faith *Evangelii Nuntiandi* was ahead of its time because it asked us to focus on what is imperative to the mission of the Church:

Evangelising is in fact the grace and vocation proper to the Church, her deepest identity. She exists in order to evangelise, that is to say, in order to preach and teach, to be a channel of the gift of grace, to reconcile sinners to God, and to perpetuate Christ's sacrifice in the Mass, which is the memorial of His death and glorious resurrection. (EN 14)

Evangelii Nuntiandi is significant because it calls all Catholics to put their faith out there and share it with others. It calls the Church itself, both hierarchy and laity, to be constantly evangelised. In particular, the role that the local church plays in evangelisation is paramount to its existence. In an age that inclined towards excessively individualistic approaches and which did not incline to faith-sharing and which did not see evangelisation as an imperative of individual churches, this document says:

The whole Church is therefore called upon to evangelise, and yet within her we have different evangelising tasks to accomplish. This diversity of services in the unity of the same mission makes up the richness and beauty of evangelisation. **(EN 66)**

Useful notes for Formation Meetings 1 and 2

On the Church as evangeliser

The Church is an evangeliser, but she begins by being evangelised herself. She is the community of believers, the community of hope lived and communicated, the community of brotherly love, and she needs to listen unceasingly to what she must believe, to her reasons for hoping, to the new commandment of love. **(EN 15)**

On the power of witness

Above all the Gospel must be proclaimed by witness. Take a Christian or a handful of Christians who, in the midst of their own community, show their capacity for understanding and acceptance, their sharing of life and destiny with other people, their solidarity with the efforts of all for whatever is noble and good. **(EN 21)**

On the place of evangelisation in our life

But evangelisation would not be complete if it did not take account of the unceasing interplay of the Gospel and man's concrete life, both personal and social. This is why evangelisation involves an explicit message, adapted to the different situations constantly being realised, about the rights and duties of every human being, about family life without which personal growth and development is hardly possible, about life in society, about international life, peace, justice and development – a message especially energetic today about liberation. **(EN 29)**

On liberation

It cannot be contained in the simple and restricted dimension of economics, politics, social or cultural life; it must envisage the whole man, in all his aspects, right up to and including his openness to absolute, even the divine Absolute. **(EN 33)**

On who is called to evangelise

But who then has the mission of evangelising? The Second Vatican Council gave a clear reply to this question: it is upon the Church that "there rests, by divine mandate, the duty of going out into the whole world and preaching the gospel to every creature" (reference to the Declaration on Religious Liberty, *Dignitatis Humanae,* 13). And in another text: "… the whole Church is missionary and the work of evangelisation is a basic duty of the People of God" (reference to the Decree on the Church's Missionary Activity, *Ad Gentes,* 35). **(EN 59)**

Formation Meeting 1

Evangelii Nuntiandi

Opening prayer

(prayed together)

Heavenly Father,
Pour forth your Holy Spirit to inspire me with these words from Holy Scripture.
Stir in my soul the desire to renew my faith and deepen my relationship with your Son,
our Lord Jesus Christ, so that I might truly believe in and live the Good News.
Open my heart to hear the Gospel and grant me the confidence
to proclaim the Good News to others.
Pour out your Spirit, so that I might be strengthened to go forth and witness to the Gospel
in my everyday life through my words and actions.
In moments of hesitation remind me:
If not me, then who will proclaim the Gospel?
If not now, then when will the Gospel be proclaimed?
If not the truth of the Gospel, then what shall I proclaim?
God our Father, I pray that through the Holy Spirit I might hear the call of the New Evangelisation to deepen my faith, grow in confidence to proclaim the Gospel and boldly witness to the saving grace of your Son, Jesus Christ, who lives and reigns with you in the unity of the Holy Spirit, one God for ever and ever.
Amen.

Welcome and introductions

As a group of people you have been invited to come together to form a team. Some of you might know each other but no doubt there will be people at the meeting you do not know (or do not know well), so we need to begin by introducing ourselves to each other. Go around the group and tell each other:

- Who you are
- What you are currently doing (your job/retired)
- If you currently do something in the parish share this with the group
- How you feel about being invited to be a part of this group
- What you hope will come about in your parish as a result of this group.

We now listen to and then reflect on a reading from scripture. The passages selected for the meetings, unless indicated, are from the ***New Revised Standard Version*** of the Bible (**NRSV**).

Scripture reading

(ask one member of the group to read the following:)

A reading from the Gospel of Mark (1:16-20)

As Jesus passed along the Sea of Galilee, he saw Simon and his brother Andrew casting a net into the lake – for they were fishermen. And Jesus said to them, "Follow me and I will make you fish for people." And immediately they left their nets and followed him. As he went a little farther, he saw James son of Zebedee and his brother John, who were in their boat mending the nets. Immediately he called them; and they left their father Zebedee in the boat with the hired men, and followed him.

Reflecting on the scripture reading

Imagine the scene – put yourself on the shore of the Sea of Galilee. Take yourself back 2000 years: you are Peter, James and John, mending your nets and perhaps discussing the day's work and hoped-for catch of the next day. Then out of the blue Jesus, an itinerant, calls you to follow him. This is more than just a challenge to leave behind income and stability, or as we might put it, to get out of our "comfort zone". Mark's account of this incident records a detail lacking in the other accounts, namely that James and John leave their father Zebedee "with the hired men". They themselves were not hired men or labourers but rather were a part of what was probably a relatively successful family business. The response of the disciples was one that could not have been taken lightly. They didn't just leave their nets behind, but a father, a wife, a boat and indeed an entire enterprise. For these disciples to follow Jesus they have to demonstrate a willingness to allow their identity, status and worth to primarily be determined in relation to him.

Jesus does not reject the earthly vocation of these men but calls them to be "fishers of people", thereby affirming their former work (fishermen) as an image of the new role to which he is calling them. Although we as Christians are not called to leave everything behind and follow Jesus, we are called to identify ourselves with Christ.

> **Questions related to the reading to share thoughts about:**
> - What does this passage from St Mark's Gospel say to you about ourselves as followers of Christ? Have we fully answered Jesus' call to follow him?
> - What should we be doing to fully understand what Jesus is asking us to do and what aren't we doing presently in order to proclaim the Gospel in our neighbourhood?

Our parish

In the opening sections of *Evangelii Nuntiandi* Pope Paul VI writes:

On this tenth anniversary of the closing of the Second Vatican Council... [We wish] to make the Church of the twentieth century ever better fitted to proclaiming the gospel to the people of the twentieth century. (EN 2)

For the remainder of today's meeting we would invite you to spend some time looking at your parish. You may not get through everything in this short survey but try not to spend too much time focused on just one area.

Let's now look openly at what kind of environment we have provided for our fellow parishioners. However, before we start, we want to stress that the purpose of this exercise is not to criticise or undermine, but to offer a springboard for what is possible for your parish in the future.

The few questions below can help us to look candidly at what kind of environment and welcome we provide, not only for the stranger at the door, but our own fellow parishioners.

A short survey of some key elements of your parish

For starters

- What is in your opinion the most successful element of your parish?
- What do you think people in your neighbourhood think about your parish?
- How would you describe the demographic of your parish?

What are the first impressions?

- Are the church grounds neat and tidy?
- Is the entrance clearly marked and brightly lit on dark nights?
- Is there a notice of service times that can be read from outside the church?
- Is the information on the porch noticeboard up-to-date?
- Is the information provided in the church porches updated regularly and are they bright and colourful, making them interesting to read?
- Is there plenty of information about parish activities and is it clear where people can get more information about activities and forthcoming events?
- If you have a car park, is it clearly signposted and is it safe for people at night?
- Does the church sound system work adequately and do you have a loop system for the hearing impaired? Are there signs informing people if you do?

- Is the church warm enough or do people have to wear coats to keep warm?
- Are toilet facilities available and easy to locate?
- Do you provide a large print newsletter or service sheet for the visually impaired?

During Formation Meeting 2 we will continue to look at our parish in terms of the welcome that we give.

Final reflection

(ask one member of the group to read this reflection for the group to end the meeting)

Dreams come and go in our lives;
far more die than become reality.
What is it in us that allows us to let go of visions
that could create new and beautiful worlds?
Why do we so easily give in to barriers?
Why do we let ourselves conform and be satisfied
   with what is?
Reaching out to a dream can be risky.
Our comfortableness can so easily be disturbed.
But, what beauty can be experienced
as we accept the challenge of a dream!
What a precious feeling to be supported, to have
   others say
"You can do it, we can do it together."
Nothing is beyond our reach if we reach out together,
if we reach out with the confidence we have,

if we are willing to persevere even in difficult times
and if we rejoice with every small step forward,
if we dream beautiful dreams
that will transform our lives, our world.
Nothing is impossible if we put aside our careful
   ways,
if we build our dreams with faith –
faith in ourselves, faith in our sisters and brothers,
and above all,
faith in our Lord God
with whom all things are possible.

(reference: Delora Hintz, ***Prayer Services for Parish Meetings*** (Mystic CT: Twenty-Third Publications, 1983), 66-67, in Donal Harrington and Julie Kavanagh, ***Prayer for Parish Groups*** (Dublin: Columba Press, 1998), 32-33)

Closing prayer

(prayed together)

Our Father who art in heaven,
hallowed be thy name.
Thy kingdom come.
Thy will be done on earth, as it is in heaven.
Give us this day our daily bread,
and forgive us our trespasses,
as we forgive those who trespass against us,
and lead us not into temptation,
but deliver us from evil. Amen.

Confirm the date and time of the next meeting.

Formation Meeting 2

Evangelii Nuntiandi

Opening prayer
(prayed together)

Heavenly Father,
Pour forth your Holy Spirit to inspire me with these
    words from Holy Scripture.
Stir in my soul the desire to renew my faith and
    deepen my relationship with your Son,
our Lord Jesus Christ, so that I might truly believe in
    and live the Good News.
Open my heart to hear the Gospel and grant me the
    confidence
to proclaim the Good News to others.
Pour out your Spirit, so that I might be strengthened
    to go forth and witness to the Gospel
in my everyday life through my words and actions.
In moments of hesitation remind me:
If not me, then who will proclaim the Gospel?
If not now, then when will the Gospel be proclaimed?
If not the truth of the Gospel, then what shall I
    proclaim?
God our Father, I pray that through the Holy Spirit
    I might hear the call of the New Evangelisation to
    deepen my faith, grow in confidence to proclaim
    the Gospel and boldly witness to the saving grace
    of your Son, Jesus Christ, who lives and reigns
with you in the unity of the Holy Spirit, one God
    for ever and ever.
Amen.

Introduction
In this meeting we are asked to look at the way in
which we view the task we are to undertake. Jesus
called the Twelve and told them he would make them
fishers of men. He didn't say that he would give them
an easy task or that they would be special and stand
out from the crowd. But there was no doubt that the
mandate he gave them was directly from him and all
he was asking them to do was to be like him.

As a Parish Evangelisation Team you are about
to undertake a task that is not an easy one and at
times it will seem an impossible one. In this meeting
we will look at ways of simply being and giving of
ourselves to the work of the Lord.

Any feedback or reflections from the previous meeting
This is a chance for the team to speak about any
matters arising from the last meeting. Depending on
time, we suggest that you take five to ten minutes to
talk to each other, first in pairs and then as a group.

Scripture reading

(ask one member of the group to read the following:)

A reading from the Gospel of Mark (6:6-13)

Then he went about among the villages teaching. He called the twelve and began to send them out two by two, and gave them authority over the unclean spirits. He ordered them to take nothing for their journey except a staff; no bread, no bag, no money in their belts; but to wear sandals and not to put on two tunics. He said to them, "Wherever you enter a house, stay there until you leave the place. If any place will not welcome you and they refuse to hear you, as you leave, shake off the dust that is on your feet as a testimony against them." So they went out and proclaimed that all should repent. They cast out many demons, and anointed with oil many who were sick and cured them.

Reflecting on the scripture reading

What kind of authority and power does the Lord want us to exercise on his behalf? Jesus gave his apostles both the power and the authority to speak and to act in his name. He commanded them to do the works which he did – and to speak the word of God – the good news of the Gospel which they received from Jesus. When Jesus spoke of power and authority he did something unheard of. He compared power and authority with love and humility. Jesus teaches us to use it for the good of our neighbour. Why does Jesus tell the apostles to travel light and with little or no provisions? Jesus wants us to be simple people, not to act in a superior way because we have been called to do his work. The Lord wants his disciples to be dependant on him and not on themselves. He wills to work through and in each of us for his glory. The Lord entrusts us with his gifts and talents.

Questions related to the reading to share thoughts about:
- How do we ensure that our parishes are places that encourage and train people to be evangelisers?
- How do we create our parishes as centres of constant missionary outreach?

Our parish

Jesus calls each and every one of us to be messengers of his holy word. As you undertake this role in your parish remember that your role as a Parish Evangelisation Team is to enable other people to know Jesus and fulfil their own mission in the Church.

At this point let's take some time to ask the question: Can we honestly say that we as a parish reach out to the whole of our community whatever their situation?

Most parishes are made up of a variety of groups. These are just a few of them:

- Young adults
- Young married couples
- Elderly married couples

- Primary school children
- Teens
- Singles: young to middle age
- Singles: elderly, living alone
- Widowed
- Single-parent families
- Newcomers
- Sick/housebound/in nursing homes
- Divorced/separated
- Remarried
- Unemployed
- Lesbian, gay, bisexual, transgender
- Ex-prisoners.

It is in this consideration of the makeup of the parish that we establish the uniqueness of the parish. In *Evangelii Nuntiandi* we are asked to consider how

The individual Churches, intimately built up not only of people but also of aspirations, of riches and limitations, of ways of praying, of loving, of looking at life and the world, which distinguish this or that human gathering, have the task of assimilating the essence of the Gospel message and of transposing it, without the slightest betrayal of its essential truth, into the language that these particular people understand, then of proclaiming it in this language. (EN 63)

If time permits, give some consideration to the above passage and ask how your parish responds to these groups in the spirit of *Evangelii Nuntiandi*.

Final reflection

(ask one member of the group to read this reflection for the group to end the meeting)

Modern culture often dictates that we focus on our needs and that if we don't then we have to sacrifice our individualism; however, that wasn't always so. Benjamin Franklin said during the American Civil War, "We must all hang together or assuredly we shall all hang separately," and more recently during the civil rights struggle in the USA, Rev. Dr Martin Luther King Jr spoke of solidarity. In his "Letter from Birmingham Jail" he stated that "Injustice anywhere is a threat to justice everywhere. We are caught in an inescapable network of mutuality."

So if we are to gather the people of God and work towards a greater understanding of his Good News then we have to understand that whatever the needs of our fellow human beings, everything we do, everything we have, is dependant upon the work of others. The food we eat, the clothes we wear, the houses we live in, are wholly dependent on the labour of others, our brother and sisters.

As Christians, Jesus challenges us to go beyond what we see as solidarity and work for a fuller understanding of the needs of others. The challenge for us at this time is to enable everyone in whatever their situation to hear and experience the work of the Spirit and to build the Kingdom with them in our world and their world.

Closing prayer
(prayed together)

Lord, make me a channel of your grace and healing love
that others may find life and freedom in you.
Free me from all other attachments
that I may joyfully pursue the things of heaven.
May I witness the joy of the Gospel both in word and
    deed.
I make this prayer through Jesus Christ our risen Lord.
Amen.

(reference: <http://www.rc.net/wcc/readings/sep21a.htm>, accessed 7 Oct. 2016)

Confirm the date and time of the next meeting.

CHAPTER FOUR

Reflecting on *Evangelii Gaudium*

Formation Meetings 3 and 4

Introduction to Meetings 3 and 4 – *Evangelii Gaudium*

(to be read before the meetings)

On the 24 November 2013 Pope Francis issued his apostolic exhortation, *Evangelii Gaudium* ("The Joy of the Gospel"). Nine months after becoming the successor to Pope Benedict XVI and the 266th Bishop of Rome, *Evangelii Gaudium* was to give Pope Francis an opportunity to respond, in part, to the final message and propositions of the 2012 Synod on the New Evangelisation and also to draw together some of the key messages for his pontificate. The document was greeted with great enthusiasm and in a short space of time it was to be seen as a blueprint mission statement, or mandate, for the Church well into the future. The document and Pope Francis' pontificate to date have generated a new fervour in the Church and for the Church, and his words and his witness are proving to be inspirational for many people. The tone and content of this document were different from the papal documents of his predecessors, but it still contained a vitally important challenge to the Church as a whole, to local parish communities and to individual Catholics.

Since *Evangelii Gaudium* we have seen the publication of many other important documents such as *Laudate Si'* ("On Care for Our Common Home") in 2015 and more recently, and very timely for the Jubilee Year of Mercy 2016, *Amoris Laetitia* ("The Joy of Love"). Each in its own right serves to re-enforce the need to evangelise and proclaim the mercy of God's love, and we will be looking in more detail at these documents and how they can be used as tools for evangelisation in subsequent chapters.

"Jesus Christ loves you; he gave his life to save you; and now he is living at your side every day to enlighten, strengthen and free you"

– Pope Francis, Evangelii Gaudium

In this chapter we offer the following as a way for parishes, groups of parishioners or individuals to reflect on specific aspects of Pope Francis' document, *Evangelii Gaudium*, using certain passages focused on some of the major themes. Reflection on these themes may help you as a Parish Evangelisation Team to evaluate some of your current parish practices and explore possible new practices in your parish communities.

Pope Francis opens *Evangelii Gaudium* with:

The joy of the gospel fills the hearts and lives of all who encounter Jesus. Those who accept his offer of salvation are set free from sin, sorrow, inner emptiness and loneliness. With Christ joy is constantly born anew. In this Exhortation I wish to encourage the Christian faithful to embark upon a new chapter of evangelisation marked by this joy, while pointing out new paths for the Church's journey in years to come. **(EG 1)**

What is this new chapter he refers to? Well our best guess would be the quote below which seems to sum up the document well:

I dream of a "missionary option", that is, a missionary impulse capable of transforming everything, so that the Church's customs, ways of doing things, times and schedules, language and structures can be suitably channelled for the evangelisation of today's world rather than for her self-preservation. **(EG 27)**

This is quite a sweeping statement! Have we as a Church been in self-preservation mode for too long and are we just maintaining, rather than being missionary? In this document Pope Francis is calling for our Church to thrive by openly choosing the missionary option in everything that we do and are. Are you able to take the term New Evangelisation and make it a new reality in your parish, enabling it to become a parish where the status quo is missionary and where evangelisation is not new but normal?

Let us take a deeper look at some of the main aspects of *Evangelii Gaudium*.

The document has several major themes and we will highlight below some of the most significant ones. Many of these are reiterated many times and in many ways throughout the document, which plainly speaks of the importance Pope Francis gives to this missionary message.

Useful notes for Formation Meetings 3 and 4

The basic proclamation of the Gospel (kerygma)

The basis of evangelisation is to share the basic message of the Gospel. As Pope Francis says:

In catechesis too, we have rediscovered the fundamental role of the first announcement or kerygma, which needs to be the centre of all evangelising activity and all efforts at Church renewal... On the lips of the catechist the first proclamation must ring out over and over: "Jesus Christ loves you; he gave his life to save you; and now he is living at your side every day to enlighten, strengthen and free you." **(EG 164)**

He goes on to note the importance of the kerygma (the basic proclamation of the Gospel) throughout the life of a Christian and to stress the personal nature of proclaiming the word of God in our individual lives.

It is first in a qualitative sense because it is the principal proclamation, the one which we must hear again and again in different ways, the one which we must announce one way or another throughout the process of catechesis, at every level and moment. (**EG 164**)

Today, as the Church seeks to experience a profound missionary renewal, there is a kind of preaching which falls to each of us as a daily responsibility. It has to do with bringing the Gospel to the people we meet, whether they be our neighbours or complete strangers. This is the informal preaching that takes place in the middle of a conversation. (**EG 127**)

He also practises what he preaches when in the third paragraph he states:

I invite all Christians, everywhere, at this very moment, to a renewed personal encounter with Jesus Christ, or at least an openness to letting him encounter them; I ask all of you to do this unfailingly each day. No one should think that this invitation is not meant for him or her since "no one is excluded from the joy brought by the Lord." (**EG 3**)

Two sources of evangelisation

Firstly, a community that evangelises knows that the Lord has taken the initiative and he has loved us first (*see* 1 John 4:19). Therefore, we have been given a mandate to move forwards and take the initiative, going out into the world to seek those who have fallen away, to stand at the crossroads to welcome the outcast.

Secondly, our evangelisation depends on theme number one: our ability to accept the Gospel into our lives.

Here we find the source and inspiration of all our efforts at evangelisation. For if we have received the love which restores meaning to our lives, how can we fail to share that love with others? (**EG 8**)

Missionary disciple

In recent year we have become familiar with the term "missionary disciple" and it is used throughout the document. The term is used boldly to emphasise the mutual importance of the need both for a relationship with our Lord and the need to go to the outskirts to the marginalised, to preach the Gospel. One thing is very clear in Pope Francis' document – every baptised member of the Catholic faith is called to evangelise and is called to be a missionary disciple.

In virtue of their baptism, all the members of the People of God have become missionary disciples (cf. Matthew 28:19). All the baptised, whatever their position in the Church or their level of instruction in the faith, are agents of evangelisation. **(EG 120)**

The parish

You will see from the document that Pope Francis spends a considerable amount of time raising awareness of how a missionary impulse would change parish life.

In all its activities the parish encourages and trains its members to be evangelisers. It is a community of communities, a sanctuary where the thirsty come to drink in the midst of their journey, and a centre of constant missionary outreach. We must admit, though, that the call to review and renew our parishes has not yet sufficed to bring them nearer to people, to make them environments of living communion and participation, and to make them completely mission-oriented. **(EG 28)**

In some people we see an ostentatious preoccupation for the liturgy, for doctrine and for the Church's prestige, but without any concern that the Gospel have a real impact on God's faithful people and the concrete needs of the present time. **(EG 95)**

Then in regard to sharing the message of the Gospel, in section 135–159 (a large section of the document), Pope Francis spends a lot of time on the subject of preaching homilies, humorously saying:

We know that the faithful attach great importance to it, and that both they and their ordained ministers suffer because of homilies: the laity from having to listen to them and the clergy from having to preach them! (EG 135)

Communal commitment

If we are to take an important message from *Evangelii Gaudium*, in our opinion, it would be that as a Parish Evangelisation Team we are called to enable, to encourage, and to journey with our fellow parishioners. Pope Francis discourages what he refers to as spiritual worldliness and it would be so easy for a team to develop a Pharisaic attitude. Pope Francis makes the point that:

Spiritual worldliness, which hides behind the appearance of piety and even love for the Church, consists in seeking not the Lord's glory but human glory and personal well-being. It is what the Lord reprimanded the Pharisees for: "How can you believe, who receive glory from one another and do not seek the glory that comes from the only God?" (John 5:44). It is a subtle way of seeking one's "own interests, not those of Jesus Christ" (Philippians 2:21). It takes on many forms, depending on the kinds of persons and groups into which it seeps. Since it is based on carefully cultivated appearances, it is not always linked to outward sin; from without, everything appears as it should be. But if it were to seep into the Church, "it would be infinitely more disastrous than any other worldliness which is simply moral". (EG 93)

This worldliness can be fuelled in two deeply interrelated ways. One is the attraction of Gnosticism, a purely subjective faith whose only interest is a certain experience or a set of ideas and bits of information which are meant to console and enlighten, but which ultimately keep one imprisoned in his or her own thoughts and feelings. The other is the self-absorbed promethean neopelagianism of those who ultimately trust only in their own powers and feel superior to others because they observe certain rules or remain intransigently faithful to a particular Catholic style from the past. A supposed soundness of doctrine or discipline leads instead to a narcissistic and authoritarian elitism, whereby instead of evangelizing one analyses and classifies others, and instead of opening the door to grace, one exhausts his or her energies in inspecting and verifying. In neither case is one really concerned about Jesus Christ or others.

These are manifestations of an anthropocentric immanentism. It is impossible to think that a genuine evangelizing thrust could emerge from these adulterated forms of Christianity. **(EG 94)**

It can be difficult to impress on Parish Evangelisation Teams how important a humility of spirit is in the work of evangelisation and it is only by taking the words directly from Pope Francis that we truly understand how we are to proceed with the role we are committed to undertake.

With *Evangelii Gaudium*, Pope Francis has set us a challenge – how will we respond as individuals and as a parish community?

Formation Meeting 3

Evangelii Gaudium

Opening prayer
(prayed together)

Lord,
guide our parish to be a community of missionary
  disciples.
Help us to heed the call of Jesus
in Matthew's Gospel and hear the great command
  of Jesus
to the apostles and thus to us the Church.
We will put into practice his command
and listen to his words.
"All authority in heaven and on earth has been given
  to me. Go therefore and make disciples of all
  nations, baptising them in the name of the Father
  and of the Son and of the Holy Spirit, teaching
  them to observe all that I have commanded you.
  And behold I am with you always to the end of
  the world."
Amen.

Introduction
Today we will spend some time looking at *Evangelii
Gaudium*. We are sure that every one of you at some
stage over the last couple of years will have either heard
about or read this apostolic exhortation. Coming

just nine months into Pope Francis' pontificate,
Evangelii Gaudium was to become Pope Francis'
call to the whole Church to be an instrument for
the New Evangelisation – a gauntlet thrown down
for us to pick up and run with and that is what we
are about to do. We will spend time today looking
at where we are now and what can be achieved if we
look at our parish in a pastoral context.

Any feedback or reflections from the previous meeting
This is a chance for the team to speak about any
matters arising from the last meeting. Depending on
time, we suggest that you take five to ten minutes to
talk to each other, first in pairs and then as a group.

Scripture reading
(ask one member of the group to read the following:)

A reading from the Gospel of Matthew (28:16-20)
Now the eleven disciples went to Galilee, to the
mountain to which Jesus had directed them. When
they saw him, they worshipped him; but some
doubted. And Jesus came and said to them, "**All
authority in heaven and on earth has been given to**

confidence and also lack of understanding to focus us on the risen Lord as their leader, this ultimately defines their future, their commission to take the word of Jesus Christ to the world. It is for all who are part of the people of God and incorporates the task of making disciples with teaching, and baptising in the name of the Father, the Son and the Holy Spirit. The mandate of the Church is to be a living, teaching witness within the world and most of all Jesus promises that he will be with his people until the end of time.

At the same time, we see that for Jesus there are no half measures. We see this when Matthew relates that Jesus' command to the disciples was to make disciples of "ALL nations teaching them to observe EVERYTHING whatsoever I commanded you and to do this because ALL authority has been given unto me." He then reassures them that "I will be with you ALWAYS even unto the end of the world." Can we say that our commitment to Jesus is as definitive as his is to us?

me. Go therefore and make disciples of **all** nations, baptising them in the name of the Father and of the Son and of the Holy Spirit, and teaching them to obey **everything** that I have commanded you. And remember, I am with you **always**, to the end of the age."

Reflecting on the scripture reading

Matthew 28:16-20 records the encounter of Jesus by the disciples and these final words of Jesus close the Gospel. Moving us from the disciples' lack of

Questions related to the reading to share thoughts about:
- What can we do to enable ourselves and our fellow parishioners to have a renewed personal relationship with Jesus Christ?
- What can we do to strengthen people's belief in their abilities to be agents of evangelisation?

Our parish

Keeping in mind that as a team you are the evangelising conscience of the parish and your remit is to encourage and enable your fellow parishioners to look at the way in which evangelising strengthens the parish for a short time, consider the following questions in the context of your parish, and in the light of these quotes from *Evangelii Gaudium*:

What I would like to propose is something much more in the line of an evangelical discernment. It is the approach of a missionary disciple an approach "nourished by the light and strength of the Holy Spirit." (EG 50)

The Church is herself a missionary disciple. (EG 40)

Questions:
- What can we do to encourage people in their everyday life to go to the outskirts, to the marginalised, to preach?
- When are the times we can best share the basic Gospel message in our parishes?

Final reflection

(ask one member of the group to read this reflection for the group to end the meeting)

We are disciples of Jesus and we follow him who is the Way, the Truth and the Life. Pope Francis in "The Joy of the Gospel" writes, "In our day Jesus' command to 'go and make disciples' echoes in the changing situations and challenges to the Church's mission of evangelisation". All of us are called to take part in this new mission "going forth". It is important to understand that our starting point is with Jesus, who is the ultimate evangeliser. He has promised to be with us until the end of the world. We must understand that God takes the lead and in this endeavour makes disciples of us all.

Closing prayer

(prayed together or as prayer with responses)

When we lack boldness in your gospel
Fill us with your Spirit, O Lord

When we lose faith in your love
Fill us with your Spirit, O Lord

When our passion flags
Fill us with your Spirit, O Lord

Then send us out, in the power of that Spirit,
To proclaim your love, justice and peace
Amen.

(from Micah 6:8)

(reference: Paula Gooder, *The Joy of the Gospel* (London: Church House Publishing, 2015), 49)

Confirm the date and time of the next meeting.

Formation Meeting 4

Evangelii Gaudium

Opening prayer
(prayed together)

Lord,
guide our parish to be a community of missionary
disciples.
Help us to heed the call of Jesus
in the Gospel and hear the great command of Jesus
to the apostles and thus to us the Church.
We will put into practice his command and listen to
his words,
"All authority in heaven and on earth has been given
to me. Go therefore and make disciples of all
nations baptising them in the name of the Father
and of the Son and of the Holy Spirit teaching
them to observe all that I have commanded you.
And behold I am with you always to the end of
the age."
Amen.

Introduction
Today we will spend some time looking again at
Evangelii Gaudium. Pope Francis goes to great
lengths in this document to focus the faithful on
the need of compassion, understanding and love
of our fellow humans. Jesus' life was one of love,
selflessness and commitment to the work of his
Father and in his doing the Father's will he showed
us that. A community that evangelises knows that
the Lord has taken the initiative and he has loved
us first (*see* 1 John 4:19). Jesus waits for us to meet
him where those in need are. In doing this we have
to look at our own humility; although we have taken
on the role of a Parish Evangelisation Team, it would
be wrong for us to feel that we are the chosen ones
that have been chosen to be the evangelisers. As the
evangelising conscience of the parish we are called to
be humble in our approach to the job we are doing
and not be seen as the Pharisees. Our role is not to
teach, but to accompany our fellow parishioners on
their journey.

Any feedback or reflections from the previous meeting
This is a chance for the team to speak about any
matters arising from the last meeting. Depending on
time, we suggest that you take five to ten minutes to
talk to each other, first in pairs and then as a group.

Scripture reading

(ask one member of the group to read the following:)

A reading from the first letter of St John (1 John 4:19-21)

We love because he first loved us. Those who say, "I love God", and hate their brothers or sisters, are liars; for those who do not love a brother or sister whom they have seen, cannot love God whom they have not seen. The commandment we have from him is this: those who love God must love their brothers and sisters also.

Reflecting on the scripture reading

As Christians we love God and we strive to love each other; but is our love a grateful reaction to God's love? Can we say, as St John tells us, we love because he loved us first, because he has given us his love? So we must perceive that by his love we are able to love. But are we able to love those who are perceived as unlovable? Pope Francis says:

Here we find the source and inspiration of all our efforts at evangelisation. For if we have received the love which restores meaning to our lives, how can we fail to share that love with others? **(EG 8)**

Also:

Pastoral ministry in a missionary style is not obsessed with the disjointed transmission of a multitude of doctrines to be insistently imposed… the message has to concentrate on the essentials, on what is most beautiful, most grand, most appealing and at the same time most necessary. The message is simplified, while losing none of its depth and truth, and thus becomes all the more forceful and convincing. **(EG 35)**

Questions related to the reading to share thoughts about:
- How do we demonstrate that God has loved us first, that God took the initiative?
- Can we name a few opportunities that the Lord puts before our parish community to recognise his presence in today's world?

Our parish

As a Christian community we are called upon to be stewards of our fellow sisters and brothers. Jesus walked amongst the poor, the marginalised, and those who were the dregs of society. In much the same way Pope Francis calls us to make this part of our mission. Now take some time to look at how your parish can honour this missionary mandate.

Questions:
- How can we encourage the people in the pews to be the ones who go out to others, to seek those who have fallen away, to stand at the crossroads and welcome the outcast?
- How do we ensure that our parish is a place that encourages and trains people to be evangelisers? And how do we create our parish as a centre of constant missionary outreach?

Final reflection

(ask one member of the group to read this reflection for the group to end the meeting)

Commitment begins in **love**. As Jesus said to Peter do you love me? So our Gospel commitment is founded in our ever-deepening love for Jesus.

Commitment is nourished by **memory**. It means frequently going back over the life, death and resurrection of Jesus, our inspiration and hope. It means often bringing back to mind our original enthusiasm for our calling.

Commitment is fired by **passion**. When we think upon our passionate God, the same passion stirs in our hearts; we feel God's own feelings for all God's creatures and all God's creation.

Commitment is sustained by **courage**. It understands that things were never going to be easy and so it trusts in the Spirit's gift of courage to help it be patient and endure, awaiting with confidence the providence of the Lord.

Commitment is lived in **solidarity**. To be called is to be gathered, to struggle is to struggle together. Commitment finds its hope and energy in the sharing of vision and experience between disciples.

Commitment is carried along by **joy.** At its core it is a deep appreciation that the Gospel is good news, indeed the best news the world could ever know.

Closing prayer

(prayed together or as prayer with responses)

Lord Jesus Christ, we hear your call to go forth into the world
Knowing you will be with us to the end of the age

We go to seek the lost, the poor and the sick
Knowing you will be with us to the end of the age

We fling wide the doors of our churches and our hearts
Knowing you will be with us to the end of the age

We offer rest to the weary and refreshment to the thirsty
Knowing you will be with us to the end of the age

And
**may the grace of our Lord Jesus Christ,
and the love of God
and the fellowship of the Holy Spirit
be with us all
evermore.
Amen.**

(reference: Paula Gooder, *The Joy of the Gospel* (London: Church House Publishing, 2015), 16)

Confirm the date and time of the next meeting.

CHAPTER FIVE

Reflecting on *Laudato Si'*

Formation Meetings 5 and 6

Introduction to Meetings 5 and 6 – *Laudato Si'*

(to be read before the meetings)

In "Catholicism and the challenge of ecology", the theologian Alister McGrath is recorded as saying, "Individual sacrifice on behalf of the environment – God's creation – can serve not only the future of the planet but as a witness to our faith." (*See* Catholic News Service <https://youtu.be/4LrIww-06_4>, accessed 17 Jan. 2017.)

If we think that Pope Francis' papal encyclical *Laudato Si'* is just about climate change then we could not be further from the truth. It is an encyclical about humanity. Pope Francis says that the natural environment suffers because we misunderstand humanity.

When human beings fail to find their true place in this world, they misunderstand themselves and end up acting against themselves. (LS 115)

In the same paragraph he then goes on to quote St John Paul II, who said:

Not only has God given the earth to man, who must use it with respect for the original good purpose for which it was given, but, man too is God's gift to man. He must therefore respect the natural and moral structure with which he has been entrusted. (LS 115, quoting John Paul II, *Centesimus Annus*)

Paul L. Younger, a Christian environmental engineer currently at the University of Glasgow, in a paper on the papal encyclical, gives a breakdown of the most common technical terms found in the main body of the text of the encyclical:

environment (158); life (112); poverty/poor (73); ecology (69); biodiversity/species/animal/plant (66); earth (58); land/soil (45); pollution (40); water (45); waste (28); consumerism (23); sustainability (22); lifestyle (21); climate (14); urban (11); air (9)

(reference: "Laudato Si': an environmental engineer reads Pope Francis", August 2015 edition of **Open House**, an independent Catholic journal)

In other words, Pope Francis in his encyclical has not focused on one single issue but has addressed the great global sustainability challenges of our times. His teachings are radical but they are timely for our world, which is at a turning point where we can no longer ignore the many issues and challenges raised by the Pope. But most importantly along with the challenges issued, Pope Francis also gives us reason for hope when he says:

Yet all is not lost. Human beings, while capable of the worst, are also capable of rising above themselves, choosing again what is good and making a new start. (LS 205)

Laudato Si' is the first encyclical in the history of the Church dedicated to the environment and ecology, dedicated to our common home, the Earth. Pope Francis covers a wide range of issues and is most certainly outspoken and comprehensive and, while *Laudato Si'* is written for the Catholic Church, once again Pope Francis has produced a document full of wisdom, spirituality and practical solutions that also speak to people outside of the Church. The encyclical has been widely praised and widely reported since its promulgation, probably more than you would expect for an explicitly religious document. The document has led to many conferences in the Catholic Church around the world, with calls for people to make their own *Laudato Si'* promise for each day, raising the question, "How will you live *Laudato Si'* today?"

Much of the document is addressed by Pope Francis to "every person living on this planet" (LS 3) with a desire to promote dialogue with all people: "In this Encyclical I would like to enter into dialogue with all people about our common home" (LS 3).

While admitting that this introduction to *Laudato Si'* and the subsequent meetings based on it have been by far the hardest to write in terms of evangelisation, it is only through a thorough reading of the document and reflection on what the Pope is teaching us that we have been able to see that there is a specifically Catholic/Christian way of viewing the environment and the issues and challenges that face us at this time. There may also be a more evangelistic motive. Pope Francis is convinced that the Church needs to do more with evangelisation and in producing this encyclical he is engaging with people who currently don't listen to the Church.

There are various ways in which the environment is relevant to our faith (and evangelisation and the work of a Parish Evangelisation Team is all about how we help people to transmit their faith in the world). We must keep in mind that firstly God created nature as an expression of his love and offered it to us in trust as faithful stewards. God's creation connects us to God. If we disconnect ourselves from creation by exploiting it rather than living in harmony with it, we separate ourselves from God.

"Human beings, while capable of the worst, are also capable of rising above themselves, choosing again what is good and making a new start"
– Pope Francis, Laudato Si'

The care of creation and the environment has long been a concern for the Church. It is found in the words of scripture (both Jewish and Christian). It is found in Catholic social teaching, especially in relation to the knock-on effects of the problems and issues for the poor and the vulnerable.

This encyclical is both liberating and empowering. It praises all those who, down the years, have engaged with the environment and tried to change people's perceptions of how we are called to be stewards of the world of our creator. It is a radical call to conversion to realise our vocation to be protectors of God's handiwork (LS 217).

This encyclical encourages more people, religious believers and non-believers alike, to engage in a respectful dialogue about how we can better fulfil our responsibilities to each other and the natural world that we share. This could well be the greatest contribution that Pope Francis makes to the changing world, of care for our common home. He stresses and describes how the poor and the natural world suffer together when people view themselves as the most important creatures in the world.

The story of St Francis of Assisi inspired Jorge Mario Bergoglio to take the name Francis when he assumed the papacy in 2013. In his speech to the representatives of the communications media on 16 March 2013 he spoke of how when the votes were being counted and had reached two thirds for him, his good friend Cardinal Cláudio Hummes, sitting next to him, gave him a hug and a kiss and said, "Don't forget the poor!"

And those words came to me: the poor the poor. Then, right away, thinking of the poor, I thought of Francis of Assisi. Then I thought of all the wars, as the votes were still being counted, till the end. Francis is also the man of peace. That is how the name came into my heart: Francis of Assisi. For me, he is the man of poverty, the man of peace, the man who loves and protects creation; these days we do not have a very good relationship with creation, do we? He is the man who gives us this spirit of peace, the poor man… How I would like a Church which is poor and for the poor! **(Pope Francis, Speech to the representatives of the communications media, 16 March 2013)**

After such an experience it was only a matter of time before the Church was to be gifted with a visionary and radical encyclical from Pope Francis on creation, the environment and the poor and vulnerable.

Pope Francis draws on the phrase "Praise be to you" (Laudato Si') which is much used in St Francis' "Canticle of Brother Sun and Sister Moon". Praise is

not usually something mentioned in environmental debates. Usually it's more about averting disaster. So where is the praise in Pope Francis' writing? Well, Pope Francis observes that rather than a problem to be solved, the world is a joyful mystery to be contemplated with gladness and praise. In *Laudato Si'* he quotes the Psalms: "The Psalms frequently exhort us to praise God the Creator" (LS 72).

In our two formation meetings inspired by *Laudato Si'* we will be looking at how we the Church, and in particular our parish communities, can bear witness to our faith and evangelise through our care for our common home.

Formation Meeting 5

Laudato Si'

Pope Francis offers the following prayer at the conclusion of *Laudato Si'* as a prayer we can share with all who believe in a God who is the all-powerful creator:

Opening prayer
(prayed together)

A prayer for our earth

All-powerful God, you are present in the whole universe
and in the smallest of your creatures.
You embrace with your tenderness all that exists.
Pour out upon us the power of your love,
that we may protect life and beauty.
Fill us with peace, that we may live
as brothers and sisters, harming no one.
O God of the poor,
help us to rescue the abandoned and forgotten of this earth,
so precious in your eyes.
Bring healing to our lives,
that we may protect the world and not prey on it,
that we may sow beauty, not pollution and destruction.
Touch the hearts
of those who look only for gain
at the expense of the poor and the earth.
Teach us to discover the worth of each thing,
to be filled with awe and contemplation,
to recognise that we are profoundly united
with every creature
as we journey towards your infinite light.
We thank you for being with us each day.
Encourage us, we pray, in our struggle
for justice, love and peace.
Amen.

(Pope Francis, **Laudato Si'**)

Introduction
The choice of a papal encyclical on the environment and care for our common home may seem a somewhat odd choice for discussion during a time of formation for a Parish Evangelisation Team. But as we stated in the introduction to this section of the formation meetings, *Laudato Si'* is an encyclical about humanity and it is in the midst of humanity that we are called to be disciples, to form other disciples and to proclaim the Gospel message; and there are various ways in which the environment is relevant to our faith (and evangelisation and the

work of a Parish Evangelisation Team is all about how we help people to transmit their faith in the world).

In fact, even before the Pope penned *Laudato Si'*, in *Evangelii Gaudium* ("The Joy of the Gospel") Pope Francis reminded us that:

An authentic faith… always involves a deep desire to change the world, to transmit values, to leave this earth somehow better than we found it. We love this magnificent planet on which God has put us, and we love the human family which dwells here, with all its tragedies and struggles, its hopes and aspirations, its strengths and weaknesses. The earth is our common home and all of us are brothers and sisters. If indeed "the just ordering of society and of the state is a central responsibility of politics", the Church "cannot and must not remain on the sidelines in the fight for justice." (EG 183)

Any feedback or reflections from the previous meeting

This is a chance for the team to speak about any matters arising from the last meeting. Depending on time, we suggest that you take five to ten minutes to talk to each other, first in pairs and then as a group.

Scripture reading

(ask one member of the group to read the following:)

A reading: Psalm 148

Praise the LORD!
Praise the Lord from the heavens;
praise him in the heights!
Praise him, all his angels;
praise him, all his host!

Praise him, sun and moon;
praise him, all you shining stars!
Praise him, you highest heavens,
and you waters above the heavens!

Let them praise the name of the LORD,
for he commanded and they were created.
He established them for ever and ever;
he fixed their bounds, which cannot be passed.

Praise the LORD from the earth,
you sea monsters and all deeps,
fire and hail, snow and frost,
stormy wind fulfilling his command!

Mountains and all hills,
fruit trees and all cedars!
Wild animals and all cattle,
creeping things and flying birds!

Kings of the earth and all peoples,
princes and all rulers of the earth!
Young men and women alike,
old and young together!

Let them praise the name of the LORD
for his name alone is exalted;

his glory is above earth and heaven.
He has raised up a horn for his people,
praise for all his faithful,
for the people of Israel who are close to him.
Praise the LORD!

Reflecting on the scripture reading

There's no denying that this psalm is about praising God. The invitation given to us is to praise the Lord at all times, and in all places. The psalm also reminds us that it is not just human beings that are to praise the Lord, but everything that has been created by God should praise the name of the Lord.

The reason why all created things are to praise the Lord is precisely because God created them. The whole cosmos is to engage in a great hymn of praise for the creative work of the Lord. With the command to the sea monsters and the different weather conditions to praise the Lord there is a feeling of this being a forerunner to St Francis' great canticle on creation.

Do we praise God enough for his great act of creation? Do we take for granted the presence of God in creation, the opportunities to see a beautiful sunset, to witness the beauty of a snowscape, to wonder at the sight of a humpback whale breaching the water (even if only on a TV screen).

This psalm tells us that all the hosts of heaven praise the Lord. Praising the Lord is a duty and a privilege. If we don't get some practice in now while on earth, we will feel rather out of place when we get to heaven.

Questions related to the reading to share thoughts about:

- Are there any phrases from Psalm 148 or the scriptures in general that particularly strike you as important in terms of our care of our common home?
- What does nature teach us about the creator? Has your own experience of creation helped you to pray or communicate with God? Do you have a special place in mind that reminds you of the wonder of God's creation?

Our parish

In the light of **Laudato Si'** and especially the two paragraphs taken from it below, let us spend some time reflecting on the questions that follow.

The universe as a whole, in all its manifold relationships, shows forth the inexhaustible riches of God. (LS 86)

Whether believers or not, we are agreed today that the earth is essentially a shared inheritance whose fruits are meant to benefit everyone. (LS 93)

Questions:

- In terms of the Catholic community in general, do environmental problems bother us? Are we so pre-occupied with other things happening in the world and in the Church that creation, the environment and the plight of the poor tend to be overlooked?

- What examples of our parish's concern for creation, the environment and the plight of the poor can we identify? Is there more that we can do?

Final reflection

(ask one member of the group to read the canticle and perhaps another member to read the reflection overleaf for the group to end the meeting)

St Francis' "Canticle of Brother Sun and Sister Moon"

Most High, all powerful, good Lord,
Yours are the praises, the glory, the honour,
and all blessing.
To You alone, Most High, do they belong,
and no man is worthy to mention Your name.
Be praised, my Lord, through all Your creatures,
especially through my lord Brother Sun,
who brings the day; and You give light through him.
And he is beautiful and radiant in all his splendour!
Of You, Most High, he bears the likeness.
Praise be You, my Lord, through Sister Moon
and the stars, in heaven You formed them
clear and precious and beautiful.
Praised be You, my Lord, through Brother Wind,
and through the air, cloudy and serene,
and every kind of weather through which
You give sustenance to Your creatures.
Praised be You, my Lord, through Sister Water,
so very useful and humble and precious
and chaste.

Praised be You, my Lord, through Brother Fire,
through whom You light the night and he is
beautiful
and playful and robust and strong.
Praised be You, my Lord, through Sister Mother Earth,
who sustains us and governs us and who produces
varied fruits with coloured flowers and herbs.
Praised be You, my Lord,
through those who give pardon for Your love,
and bear infirmity and tribulation.
Blessed are those who endure in peace
for by You, Most High, they shall be crowned.
Praised be You, my Lord,
through our Sister Bodily Death,
from whom no living man can escape.
Woe to those who die in mortal sin.
Blessed are those whom death will
find in Your most holy will,
for the second death shall do them no harm.
Praise and bless my Lord,
and give Him thanks
and serve Him with great humility.
AMEN.

St Francis reminds us in his canticle that our common home is like a sister with whom we share our life and a beautiful mother who opens her arms to embrace us. St Francis praises God for some of the wonders of the material world. He believed that everything in the natural world was a gift from God and as such deserved to be appreciated and valued. Because of this, one of the most charming and unique features of the canticle is the way in which he refers to the sun, wind, air and fire as his brothers and to the moon, stars, earth, water and death as his sisters. St Francis has a high regard for God as creator and for all creations that come from him.

In his canticle St Francis touches on several major themes of Christian spirituality. Firstly, the overarching theme for him in much of his life and work is how God's love is shown in creation. Francis expresses his love for God, his Father and provider, as well as his love for all of his brothers and sisters in creation.

Suffering is another important theme for St Francis. Although neither Jesus nor the Cross is explicitly mentioned in the canticle, St Francis tells us that suffering will come and those who endure it in peace will be blessed.

Glory and the Light of God is the most central theme in this piece. The very first thing St Francis does is to attribute all glory and honour to God. St Francis is overwhelmed by the glory of God, seen in the beauty of his creation. He acknowledges that even in their beauty and splendour these earthly things are mere shadows of the brilliance and glory of their creator.

Pope Francis offers the following prayer at the conclusion of **Laudato Si'** as a prayer in which we Christians ask for inspiration to take up the commitment to creation set before us by the Gospel of Jesus.

Closing prayer
(prayed together)

A Christian prayer in union with creation

Father, we praise you with all your creatures.
They came forth from your all-powerful hand;
they are yours, filled with your presence and your
    tender love.
Praise be to you!

Son of God, Jesus,
through you all things were made.
You were formed in the womb of Mary our Mother,
you became part of this earth,
and you gazed upon this world with human eyes.
Today you are alive in every creature
in your risen glory.
Praise be to you!

Holy Spirit, by your light
you guide this world towards the Father's love
and accompany creation as it groans in travail.

You also dwell in our hearts
and you inspire us to do what is good.
Praise be to you!

Triune Lord, wondrous community of infinite love,
teach us to contemplate you
in the beauty of the universe,
for all things speak of you.
Awaken our praise and thankfulness
for every being that you have made.
Give us the grace to feel profoundly joined
to everything that is.
God of love, show us our place in this world
as channels of your love
for all the creatures of this earth,
for not one of them is forgotten in your sight.
Enlighten those who possess power and money
that they may avoid the sin of indifference,
that they may love the common good, advance the
    weak,
and care for this world in which we live.
The poor and the earth are crying out.
O Lord, seize us with your power and light,
help us to protect all life,
to prepare for a better future,
for the coming of your Kingdom
of justice, peace, love and beauty.
Praise be to you!
Amen.

(Pope Francis, *Laudato Si'*)

Confirm the date and time of the next meeting.

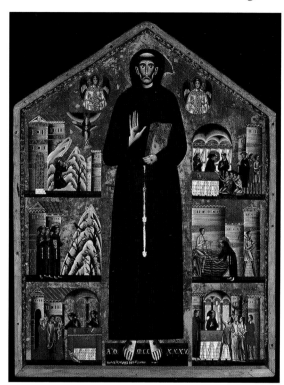

Formation Meeting 6

Laudato Si'

We repeat the opening prayer from the last meeting, which as you might remember is by Pope Francis, who offers this prayer at the conclusion of ***Laudato Si'*** as a prayer we can share with all who believe in a God who is the all-powerful creator.

Opening prayer
(prayed together)

A prayer for our earth

All-powerful God, you are present in the whole universe
and in the smallest of your creatures.
You embrace with your tenderness all that exists.
Pour out upon us the power of your love,
that we may protect life and beauty.
Fill us with peace, that we may live
as brothers and sisters, harming no one.
O God of the poor,
help us to rescue the abandoned and forgotten of this earth,
so precious in your eyes.
Bring healing to our lives,
that we may protect the world and not prey on it,
that we may sow beauty, not pollution and destruction.

Touch the hearts
of those who look only for gain
at the expense of the poor and the earth.
Teach us to discover the worth of each thing,
to be filled with awe and contemplation,
to recognise that we are profoundly united
with every creature
as we journey towards your infinite light.
We thank you for being with us each day.
Encourage us, we pray, in our struggle
for justice, love and peace.
Amen.

(Pope Francis, **Laudate Si'**)

Introduction
Having looked at one aspect of ***Laudato Si'*** in our last meeting, the care of creation, we now turn our attention to another important aspect of the document, that is, the implications of a lack of care for the environment on the poor of the world. Ultimately, the wealthy nations of the world will feel the impact of the issues Pope Francis raises in the encyclical less than the developing nations of the world.

At the start of your last meeting we referred to this encyclical as an encyclical about humanity. As we progress through this meeting we must keep at the forefront of our discussions and reflections the fact that it is in the midst of humanity that we are called to be disciple, to form other disciples, and to proclaim the Gospel message. Hopefully by now, several meetings into our time of formation, we are seeing how there are various different ways in which we put evangelisation into practice and the environment is certainly relevant to our faith.

Any feedback or reflections from the previous meeting

This is a chance for the team to speak about any matters arising from the last meeting. Depending on time, we suggest that you take five to ten minutes to talk to each other, first in pairs and then as a group.

Scripture readings

(ask one member of the group to read the first reading and perhaps another member to read the second reading)

A reading from the Gospel of Luke (7:11-17)

Soon afterwards he went to a town called Nain, and his disciples and a large crowd went with him. As he approached the gate of the town, a man who had died was being carried out. He was his mother's only son, and she was a widow; and with her was a large crowd from the town. When the Lord saw her, he had compassion for her and said to her, "Do not weep." Then he came forward and touched the bier, and the bearers stood still. And he said, "Young man, I say to you, rise!" The dead man sat up and began to speak, and Jesus gave him to his mother. Fear seized all of them; and they glorified God, saying, "A great prophet has risen among us!" and "God has looked favourably on his people!" This word about him spread throughout Judea and all the surrounding country.

A reading from the Gospel of Luke (18:35-43)

As he approached Jericho, a blind man was sitting by the roadside begging. When he heard a crowd going by, he asked what was happening. They told him, "Jesus of Nazareth is passing by." Then he shouted, "Jesus, Son of David, have mercy on me!" Those who were in front sternly ordered him to be quiet; but he shouted even more loudly, "Son of David, have mercy on me!" Jesus stood still and ordered the man to be brought to him; and when he came near, he asked him, "What do you want me to do for you?" He said, "Lord, let me see again." Jesus said to him, "Receive your sight; your faith has saved you." Immediately he regained his sight and followed him, glorifying God; and all the people, when they saw it, praised God.

Reflecting on the scripture readings

The two passages we have just read and listened to speak of Jesus' compassion to the poor, the suffering and the hopeless in the eyes of the world.

Interestingly in the first passage, Jesus immediately took action upon seeing the plight of the widow, who had no husband to care for her, and now she was about to bury her only son. She was in a hopeless situation, with her husband and only son dead. Who was going to care for her? Surely she was destined for the same journey her son was now on, with no one to look after her. But Jesus always gives hope and shows his compassion.

In the second passage, it is once more someone in a hopeless situation (in worldly terms) who becomes the recipient of Jesus' compassion and healing powers. The people around him try to silence his cries for help from Jesus, Son of David. But he was a determined man and this only made him cry out all the louder! Jesus restoring the blind man's sight leads to two very distinct reactions. Firstly, the former blind man followed Jesus, praising God, and secondly, the people who witnessed this miracle, who had been trying to silence the blind man, were now also drawn into praising God. Acts of kindness and compassion lead people to praise God – our own acts of kindness (either individually or as a parish community) should lead others to praise God.

> **Questions related to the reading to share thoughts about:**
> - Do we seek to do something that can alleviate the pain and suffering of the poor?
> - Do we listen to the voice of the poor in our world?

Our parish

Many of the poor live in areas particularly affected by phenomena related to global warming and their means of subsistence are largely dependant on natural reserves and eco-systemic services such as agriculture, fishing and forestry. They have no other financial activities or resources which can enable them to adapt to climate change or to face natural disasters, and their access to social services and protection is very limited. For example, changes in climate to which animals and plants cannot adapt lead them to migrate; this in turn affects the livelihood of the poor, who are then forced to leave their homes with great uncertainty for their future and that of their children. There has been a tragic rise in the number of migrants seeking to flee from the growing poverty caused by environmental degradation. They are not recognised by international conventions as refugees; they bear the loss of the lives they have left behind without enjoying any legal protection whatsoever. Sadly, there is widespread indifference to such suffering, which is even now taking place throughout our world. Our lack of response to these tragedies, involving our brothers and sisters, points to the loss of that sense of responsibility for our fellow men and women upon which all civil society is founded.

Today, however, we have to realise that a true ecological approach **always** becomes a social approach; "it must integrate questions of justice in debates on the environment so as to hear **both the cry of the earth and the cry of the poor**" (LS 49).

Questions:
- How can we ensure that within our parish community there is no indifference to the cry of the poor, both locally and in the developing world?
- Why and how does our faith call us to respond?

Final reflection and closing prayer

(ask one member of the group to read this reflection for the group to end the meeting)

People are often unreasonable, irrational and self-centred.
Forgive them anyway.

If you are kind people may accuse you of selfish ulterior motives.
Be kind anyway.

If you are successful, you will win some unfaithful friends and some genuine enemies.
Succeed anyway.

If you are honest and sincere, people may deceive you.
Be honest and sincere anyway.

What you spend years creating others could destroy overnight.
Create anyway.

If you find serenity and happiness some may be jealous.
Be happy anyway.

The good you do today will often be forgotten.
Do good anyway.

Give the best you have and it will never be enough.
Give your best anyway.

In the final analysis it is between you and God.
It was never between you and them anyway.

(This prayer was found written on the wall in St Teresa of Kolkata's home for children in Kolkata and is accredited to her. St Teresa of Kolkata is also known as Mother Teresa of Calcutta)

Confirm the date and time of the next meeting.

CHAPTER SIX

Reflecting on *Amoris Laetitia*

Formation Meetings 7 and 8

Introduction to Meetings 7 and 8 – *Amoris Laetitia*

(to be read before the meetings)

Papal encyclicals and apostolic exhortations do not usually cause a sensation or have large sales numbers. However, *Evangelii Gaudium* has sold more than 42,000 copies in the UK alone. *Laudato Si'* has sold over 15,500 in the UK alone and we don't have any figures for *Amoris Laetitia* as yet. Since the beginning of his papacy Pope Francis has changed many people's views of the Catholic Church, perhaps through his simple but at the same time powerful teachings on how to live out our faith in the world in which we live.

Amoris Laetitia is Pope Francis' encyclical issued as a result of his reflection on the two meetings of the Synods on the Family (2014 and 2015) and is a response to the current situation of families in today's world and in today's Church.

It is a document written specifically for the Catholic Church and whilst recognising that there are difficult situations and questions, it does not claim to give all the answers. With this encyclical Pope Francis is once again challenging the Church to look at itself, to look at the lives of its members and also to look at the possibilities of healing some of the hurt that people have in their lives. His hope is that the reading of the encyclical will encourage people to see new opportunities.

It is my hope that, in reading this text, all will feel called to love and cherish family life, for families are not a problem; they are first and foremost an opportunity. (AL 7)

This statement points to the undeniable fact that this encyclical is another document from Pope Francis about evangelisation. Time and time again Pope Francis (in this document and in other documents) is challenging the Church to do more than simply repeat the *Catechism*. He is constantly challenging the Church to model ourselves on Jesus in our living, our leading, our ministry and all of our pastoral activity. He tells us that we need to find the right language, arguments, and forms of witness, especially now in the messiness of our present world situation.

Pope Francis has spoken on many occasions of how he feels that the Church must be like a field hospital. In the case of marriage and family life he is urging the Church to meet couples and families whose lives perhaps fall short of the ideal that the Church presents where they are not where the Church would like them to be.

Pope Francis, quoting from the final report of the 2014 and 2015 Synods on the Family, says:

The Church must accompany with attention and care the weakest of her children, who show signs of a wounded and troubled love, by restoring in them hope and confidence, like the beacon of a lighthouse in a port or a torch carried among the people to enlighten those who have lost their way or who are in the midst of a storm. Let us not forget that the Church's task is often like that of a field hospital. (AL 291)

Pope Francis is not simply an idealist. He is aware that in our day families experience many anxieties because of consumerism, migration, unemployment, a throwaway culture of individualism, sickness and poverty, to name but a few factors. But he sees the opportunities that are before the Church to make a difference in people's lives and help them to experience the joy of love once more. As well as evangelisation and joy being central messages in this document, mercy also plays a large part, as Pope Francis sees how the Church must constantly be an agent of mercy in the world. All of this demands new ways of being a missionary Church seeking new forms of missionary creativity.

I thank God that many families, which are far from considering themselves perfect, live in love, fulfil their calling and keep moving forward, even if they fall many times along the way. The Synod's reflections show us that there is no stereotype of the ideal family, but rather a challenging mosaic made up of many different realities with all their joys, hopes and problems. The situations that concern us are challenges. We should not be trapped into wasting our energy in doleful laments, but rather seek new forms of missionary creativity. In every situation that presents itself the Church is conscious of the need to offer a word of truth and hope. (AL 57)

Pope Francis talks of the Church as being a family of families, being constantly enriched by the lives of all those domestic churches, our families. In this he challenges us to reflect on the interplay between the family and the Church and in doing so we will discover a precious gift for the Church in our time.

The Church is good for the family and the family is good for the Church. (AL 87)

In establishing a Parish Evangelisation Team, you must be conscious of the importance of marriage and family life, which plays such a large part in the life of our parishes, and of the many opportunities that are presented to us to help strengthen family life, to heal the hurts of family life, and to help prepare people to live out their experience of the joy of love in the world.

Chapter four of **Amoris Laetitia** presents us with a beautiful meditation on love in marriage through using the definition of love in a reading that is proclaimed at many weddings from St Paul's first letter to the Church in Corinth (1 Corinthians 12:31 – 13:8): "Love is always patient and kind; it is never jealous".

This meditation on love, reflected upon as a Parish Evangelisation Team, could help to shape your own renewed views on love, marriage and family life and help prepare us to then seriously reflect on some of the pastoral perspectives that Pope Francis offers in chapter six, including our pastoral care of families' preparation for marriage, encouraging family prayer, pastoral care for those who are separated, divorced, abandoned or remarried and for grieving families at times of bereavement. There are so many opportunities for us to reach out and evangelise families and encourage and enable families to evangelise others.

Archbishop Joseph Kurtz, the President of the US conference of Catholic Bishops, during a press conference on **Amoris Laetitia**, said that Pope Francis is attempting to help people encounter Jesus and feel the love of God, and he described this latest apostolic exhortation as a love letter to families that invites all people to never stop growing in love.

Cardinal Donald Wuerl of Washington DC said, "It's a beautiful apostolic exhortation because it doesn't say here are the answers to everything."

We began this section of the chapter on **Amoris Laetitia** by saying that this encyclical is another document from Pope Francis about evangelisation. If there is any doubt about its clear message on evangelisation simply take a look at some of the passages that refer to evangelisation in the document (which will also be a useful quick reference for discussion in the formation meetings, and once the Parish Evangelisation Team is established).

Useful notes for Formation Meetings 7 and 8

On the Gospel message

This message [the kerygma] has to occupy the centre of all evangelising activity. It is the first and most important proclamation which we must hear again and again in different ways, and which we must always announce in one form or another. (AL 58)

On the family in the world

Christian families should never forget that "faith does not remove us from the world but draws us more deeply into it… Each of us, in fact, has a special role in preparing for the coming of God's kingdom in our world". Families should not see themselves as a refuge from society, but instead go forth from their homes in a spirit of solidarity with others. In this way, they become a hub for integrating persons into society and a point of contact between the public and private spheres. (AL 181)

On the witness of families

By their witness as well as their words, families speak to others of Jesus. They pass on the faith, they arouse a desire for God and they reflect the beauty of the Gospel and its way of life. (AL 184)

On evangelisation in the family

Enabling families to take up their role as active agents of the family apostolate calls for "an effort at evangelisation and catechesis inside the family." (AL 200)

On the opportunity to evangelise during a wedding

Frequently, the celebrant speaks to a congregation that includes people who seldom participate in the life of the Church, or who are members of other Christian denominations or religious communities. The occasion thus provides a valuable opportunity to proclaim the Gospel of Christ. (AL 216)

On liturgy and devotion as a means of evangelisation

Liturgies, devotional practices and the Eucharist celebrated for families, especially on the wedding anniversary, were mentioned as vital factors in fostering evangelisation through the family. (AL 223)

On pastoral care and evangelisation

Nowadays, pastoral care for families has to be fundamentally missionary, going out to where people are. We can no longer be like a factory, churning out courses that for the most part are poorly attended. (AL 230)

On evangelisation of the divorced and remarried

It is important that the divorced who have entered a new union should be made to feel part of the Church. "They are not excommunicated" and they should not be treated as such, since they remain part of the ecclesial community. These situations "require careful discernment and respectful accompaniment. Language or conduct that might lead them to feel discriminated against should be avoided, and they should be encouraged to participate in the life of the community. The Christian community's care of such persons is not to be considered a weakening of its faith and testimony to the indissolubility of marriage; rather, such care is a particular expression of its charity." **(AL 243)**

In times of bereavement

To turn our backs on a grieving family would show a lack of mercy, mean the loss of a pastoral opportunity, and close the door to other efforts at evangelisation. **(AL 253)**

On family catechesis

Family catechesis is of great assistance as an effective method in training young parents to be aware of their mission as the evangelisers of their own family. **(AL 287)**

On family prayer

It is essential that children actually see that, for their parents, prayer is something truly important. Hence moments of family prayer and acts of devotion can be more powerful for evangelisation than any catechism class or sermon. **(AL 288)**

On missionary families

The work of handing on the faith to children in the sense of facilitating its expression and growth, helps the whole family in its evangelizing mission. It naturally begins to spread the faith to all around them, even outside of the family circle. Children who grew up in missionary families often become missionaries themselves; growing up in warm and friendly families, they learn to relate to the world in this way, without giving up their faith or their convictions. **(AL 289)**

On the family as an agent of evangelisation

The family is thus an agent of pastoral activity through its explicit proclamation of the Gospel and its legacy of varied forms of witness, namely solidarity with the poor, openness to a diversity of people, the protection of creation, moral and material solidarity with other families, including those most in need, commitment to the promotion of the common good and the transformation of unjust social structures, beginning in the territory in which the family lives, through the practice of the corporal and spiritual works of mercy. **(AL 290)**

On welcome

Led by the Spirit, the family circle is not only open to life by generating it within itself, but also by going forth and spreading life by caring for others and seeking their happiness. This openness finds particular expression in hospitality, which the word of God eloquently encourages: "Do not neglect to show hospitality to strangers, for thereby some have entertained angels unawares" (Hebrews 13:2). When a family is welcoming and reaches out to others, especially the poor and the neglected, it is "a symbol, witness and participant in the Church's motherhood". Social love, as a reflection of the Trinity, is what truly unifies the spiritual meaning of the family and its mission to others, for it makes present the kerygma in all its communal imperatives. The family lives its spirituality precisely by being at one and the same time a domestic church and a vital cell for transforming the world. **(AL 324)**

Formation Meeting 7

Amoris Laetitia

Opening prayer
(prayed together)

We pray to you, God of heaven and earth,
in wonder and thanks
that you have reached out to us,
dreaming and risking.
We pray through your Son Jesus who,
never satisfied with what is,
endured hardships the mind could not anticipate.
We pray in your Spirit,
released into the world by your dream for us,
who teaches us that nothing is beyond our collective
    reach.
May your Spirit inspire us
with the confidence not to bury our talents,
but to give ourselves unreservedly to the dreams
that will transform our lives.
Amen.

(reference: Donal Harrington and Julie Kavanagh, *Prayer for Parish Groups* (Dublin: Columba Press, 1998), 33)

Introduction
In our meeting today we are inviting you to look at your parish in terms of outreach to families and those experiencing difficult times in family life. Family life is not a problem for the Church, rather it is an opportunity for the Church to reach out, showing the love of God and demonstrating acts of human compassion and support.

Any feedback or reflections from the previous meeting
This is a chance for the team to speak about any matters arising from the last meeting. Depending on time, we suggest that you take five to ten minutes to talk to each other, first in pairs and then as a group.

Scripture reading
(ask one member of the group to read the following:)

A reading from the first letter of St Paul to the Corinthians (1 Corinthians 12:31 – 13:10)
Be ambitious for the higher gifts.
And I am going to show you a way that is better than
    any of them.
If I have all the eloquence of men or of angels, but
    speak without love,
I am simply a gong booming or a cymbal clashing.
If I have the gift of prophecy,

understanding all the mysteries there are, and
    knowing everything,
and if I have faith in all its fullness, to move
    mountains,
but without love, then I am nothing at all.
If I give away all that I possess, piece by piece,
and if I even let them take my body to burn it,
but am without love, it will do me no good whatever.

Love is always patient and kind; it is never jealous;
love is never boastful or conceited; it is never rude
    or selfish;
it does not take offence, and is not resentful.
Love takes no pleasure in other people's sins but
    delights in the truth;
it is always ready to excuse, to trust, to hope,
and to endure whatever comes.

Love does not come to an end.
But if there are gifts of prophecy,
the time will come when they must fail;
or the gift of languages, it will not continue for ever;
and knowledge – for this, too, the time will come
    when this must fail.
For our knowledge is imperfect and our prophesying
    is imperfect;
but once perfection comes, all imperfect things will
    disappear.

(from the *Jerusalem Bible*)

Reflecting on the scripture reading

Pope Francis in (*Amoris Laetitia*) "The Joy of Love" encourages us to think more deeply about St Paul's passage, outlining some aspects of true love, because it can lead us to think more deeply about the relevance and necessity of true love in every family.

St Paul wants his listeners to understand that love is about more than feelings. It is about something that is put into action. It is about doing good and making a difference. To truly live love in our world is a challenge. It is perhaps the forgiveness side of love or the not bearing grudges or resentment that can be so difficult. No one can say that it is easy to forgive; it requires a great deal of sacrifice and putting others before ourselves. Within a family (of people or of the Church) there needs to be that willingness to be generous with love and mercy, for in exercising the gift of forgiveness we are liberated and those we forgive are liberated also. We are all then able to live the joy of love.

God's love is the model we must imitate: total, unconditional and free. It is life-giving and life-transforming. Our parishes are called to be life-giving and life-transforming. When people see our love for one another put into action, they may be drawn into enquiring about the Church, revitalised in their faith, or simply they may open themselves up to a personal encounter with the Lord.

Questions related to the reading to share thoughts about:

- What would you say is the hardest truth from the scripture passage above to live out in our everyday life?
- Would you describe your parish as being a parish that is life-giving and life-transforming and how is this demonstrated in everyday parish life?

Our parish

In *Amoris Laetitia,* Pope Francis highlights many different groups of people in the Church: the bereaved, single people, single parents, the widowed, the divorced, the separated, the re-married, those preparing for marriage and the newly married. We have selected just two areas to which Pope Francis is drawing our attention:

On pastoral care and evangelisation

Nowadays, pastoral care for families has to be fundamentally missionary, going out to where people are. We can no longer be like a factory, churning out courses that for the most part are poorly attended. (AL 230)

On liturgy and devotion as a means of evangelisation

Liturgies, devotional practices and the Eucharist celebrated for families, especially on the wedding anniversary, were mentioned as vital factors in fostering evangelisation through the family. (AL 223)

One of the key messages of Pope Francis is to go out to the peripheries to meet people where they are. This is the meaning of the quotation above: that our outreach to families means that we can no longer simply expect them to come to us. Instead, we the Church in the local community must be going out to them. This means that we need to get to know the families that make up our parish.

Question:
- As time goes on in our parishes, we will find ourselves being the recipients of more and more families who are displaced refugees and migrants, who have no family of their own to support them. How can we befriend them and help them?

We chose the second passage from *Amoris Laetitia* that mentions the liturgy because at all times liturgy has the power to evangelise (when it is celebrated well, is meaningful and speaks to people where they are). We also selected a passage that mentions a missionary-focused approach to families, primarily because this is possibly a large area with great potential for growth in our parishes.

Question:
- What are we doing/could we be doing to support and welcome those who are separated divorced/re-married so that they can play as full a part as possible in the life of the community?

Final reflection

(ask one member of the group to read this reflection for the group to end the meeting)

Marriage and family doesn't always get a good press. Is Christian love and marriage any different to the secular interpretations of it? The answer would have to be yes, because we recognise the divine origins of love at work in our lives.

In the film of Louis de Bernières' *Captain Corelli's Mandolin* (Universal Pictures, 2001), Dr Lannis says:

"When you fall in love it is a temporary madness. It erupts like an earthquake and then it subsides and

when it subsides, you have to make a decision. You have to work out whether your roots have become so entwined together that it is inconceivable that you should ever part. Because this is what love is.

"Love itself is what is left over when being in love has burned away. It doesn't sound very exciting does it? But it is."

Dr Lannis is simply trying to help his daughter see that marriage is a real act of will, a commitment which transcends the usual talk of love which we read about in magazines and hear in songs. He speaks from experience.

Closing prayer
(prayed together)

Prayer to the Holy Family

Jesus, Mary and Joseph,
in you we contemplate
the splendour of true love;
to you we turn with trust.

Holy Family of Nazareth,
grant that our families too
may be places of communion and prayer,
authentic schools of the Gospel
and small domestic churches.

Holy Family of Nazareth,
may families never again experience
violence, rejection and division;
may all who have been hurt or scandalised
find ready comfort and healing.
Holy Family of Nazareth,
make us once more mindful
of the sacredness and inviolability of the family,
and its beauty in God's plan.

Jesus, Mary and Joseph
Graciously hear our prayer.
Amen.

(Pope Francis, *Amoris Laetitia*)

Confirm the date and time of the next meeting.

Formation Meeting 8

Amoris Laetitia

Opening prayer
(prayed together)

We pray to you, God of heaven and earth,
in wonder and thanks
that you have reached out to us,
dreaming and risking.
We pray through your Son Jesus who,
never satisfied with what is,
endured hardships the mind could not anticipate.
We pray in your Spirit,
released into the world by your dream for us,
who teaches us that nothing is beyond our collective
   reach.
May your Spirit inspire us
with the confidence not to bury our talents,
but to give ourselves unreservedly to the dreams
that will transform our lives.
Amen.

(reference: Donal Harrington and Julie Kavanagh, ***Prayer for Parish Groups*** (Dublin: Columba Press, 1998), 33)

Introduction
During this meeting we will continue to look at our parish but especially in relation to families. In this time of formation we have been opening up areas that your team can come back to after the time of formation and involve other people from the parish in exploring these issues. This is what we are doing also in this final formation meeting.

In Chapter Seven there are resources to enable the call to action: the **parish audit** and the **action plan**, material that will enable you to continue exploring how your parish can continue to move forward in witnessing to and proclaiming the Gospel. In Chapter Eight we talk about social media, ranging from the parish website to emails, Twitter and Facebook. Social media can be useful in the task of evangelisation.

Any feedback or reflections from the previous meeting
This is a chance for the team to speak about any matters arising from the last meeting. Depending on time, we suggest that you take five to ten minutes to talk to each other, first in pairs and then as a group.

Scripture reading

(ask one member of the group to read the following:)

A reading from the Gospel of Luke (2:39-52)

When they had finished everything required by the law of the Lord, they returned to Galilee, to their own town of Nazareth. The child grew and became strong, filled with wisdom; and the favour of God was upon him.

Now every year his parents went to Jerusalem for the festival of the Passover. And when he was twelve years old, they went up as usual for the festival. When the festival was ended and they started to return, the boy Jesus stayed behind in Jerusalem, but his parents did not know it. Assuming that he was in the group of travellers, they went a day's journey. Then they started to look for him among their relatives and friends. When they did not find him, they returned to Jerusalem to search for him.

After three days they found him in the temple, sitting among the teachers, listening to them and asking them questions. And all who heard him were amazed at his understanding and his answers. When his parents saw him they were astonished; and his mother said to him, "Child, why have you treated us like this? Look, your father and I have been searching for you in great anxiety." He said to them, "Why were you searching for me? Did you not know that I must be in my Father's house?" But they did not understand what he said to them. Then he went down with them and came to Nazareth, and was obedient to them. His mother treasured all these things in her heart. And Jesus increased in wisdom and in years, and in divine and human favour.

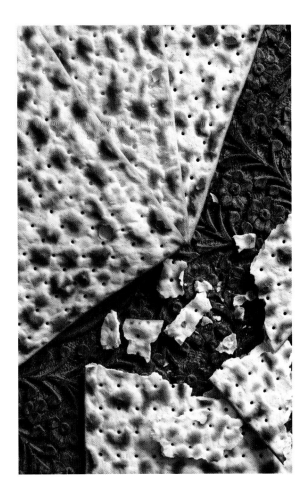

Reflecting on the scripture reading

Is it possible to say that Jesus had a normal childhood? How many parents have experienced a few seconds of panic when they lose sight of their child in the shopping centre? Mary and Joseph presumed that Jesus, on the way back from Jerusalem, was travelling with members of the extended family. It's hard to imagine the terror that they must have been feeling when Jesus was nowhere to be found in the caravan of pilgrims.

Very few children at the same age as Jesus when he went missing in the Temple would sit with academics asking questions and dialoguing with them. He knew that he must be about his Father's work, but he also grew to understand that he still had much to learn from Mary and Joseph and from a family life surrounded by his extended family and his local community in Nazareth. After Jesus went home to Nazareth we are told that he grew in wisdom in stature and in favour with God and with people.

Questions related to the reading to share thoughts about:

- How can we ensure that the children in our parishes in and through their family life grow in wisdom, stature and favour with God and with people?
- How can we support any parents who experience times of trauma or pain when bringing up a family?

Our parish

Here are some questions for you to consider with regard to how your parish supports families. In Chapter Seven you will find plenty of ideas for family ministry. Obviously it is not expected that a parish should offer all that is listed in that chapter. The important point is that we create a parish community where families feel that they belong, whether they are passing through or staying for many years.

Questions:

- Is our parish the kind of environment that actively supports parents/carers/families?
- Do we do what Pope Francis asks us to do at the end of **Amoris Laetitia** when he says, "Let us make this journey as families, let us keep walking together", and how does this manifest itself in your parish?

Final reflection

(ask one member of the group to read this reflection for the group to end the meeting)

Homelessness is a major problem in our country. On the streets of our towns and cities there are thousands of people, many of them young, who have nowhere to call home. The many refugees and asylum seekers, whilst having somewhere to shelter, are still homeless because of the uncertainty of their situation. There are many people who are spiritually homeless; also people who have no faith-community around them, or no place to gather with other people of faith where they can also experience tranquillity.

The Church formed by Jesus Christ is called to be a home for everyone. All must be made welcome. The Church must be a place where people feel loved and respected: a place of understanding and tolerance, a place of healing, reconciliation and mercy. The challenge laid at our door is the challenge of conversion of ourselves first, which will then lead to the conversion of others.

Closing prayer
(prayed together)

Prayer to the Holy Family

Jesus, Mary and Joseph,
in you we contemplate
the splendour of true love;
to you we turn with trust.

Holy Family of Nazareth,
grant that our families too
may be places of communion and prayer,
authentic schools of the Gospel
and small domestic churches.
Holy Family of Nazareth,

may families never again experience
violence, rejection and division;
may all who have been hurt or scandalised
find ready comfort and healing.

Holy Family of Nazareth,
make us once more mindful
of the sacredness and inviolability of the family,
and its beauty in God's plan.

Jesus, Mary and Joseph
Graciously hear our prayer.
Amen.

(Pope Francis, **Amoris Laetitia**)

Looking ahead

This is the point at which the time of formal formation ceases and you will turn your attention to the work of helping form your parish into a missionary parish. The chapters that follow will give some tools to help in the work you are endeavouring to undertake. We hope that in the weeks and months ahead your work will bear fruit and you and your parish will experience the **joy** of the Gospel that Pope Francis calls us all to.

CHAPTER SEVEN
(resources)

A call to action (post-formation meeting):

Parish audit and action plan

"However many holy words you read, however many you speak, what good will they do you if you do not act upon them?"

– Buddha

A call to action

This is where you are at the moment, but in order to focus your minds now on the next step, or "a call to action", it would be beneficial to consider a passage from our first book, **Welcome to Witness** (Chawton: Redemptorist Publications, 2014), page 43:

Before we can take up this challenge of reaching out to others, of evangelisation, we have a more difficult task, that of evangelising the evangelised. Most Catholic parishes are wonderful places where families live and grow in their faith. In such communities, each generation can look with affection and warmth at the parish that gave them the foundation on which to build their faith.

Alternatively, they can look back at an experience of parish that they would not put their children through, with enduring memories of a cold draughty church and an even colder response to their developing faith needs. Unfortunately, the joy of Jesus that Pope Francis speaks to us about is not always the experience that we remember.

With this is in mind, your call to action should start with taking a candid look at your parish. In doing so you can think about what kind of environment and welcome you have provided for your fellow parishioners, to say nothing of the stranger at the door. However, before you start, we want to stress that the purpose of this exercise is not to criticise or undermine, but to offer a springboard for what is possible for your parish in the future. This exercise will help you as a team to have some understanding of what you are called to do and should also be a reminder that you are not the ones doing all the work. Here we will provide some parish audit pointers as a suggested place to start. Your parish may find an alternative way of working through the surveys. That is fine: each parish reaches the destination by choosing their own path.

The following is a guide to how to get the most out of the task ahead. We suggest that the materials which follow can be used over several meetings of the Parish Evangelisation Team so that you can consider your findings and also consider the people you can enlist or contact in relation to developing the new ideas.

1. Perhaps over refreshments, look at the Parish audits. Be honest! Ensure everyone has a copy in order to briefly record their answers.
2. While completing the audits it may be necessary to take some time to look around the church and its grounds.
3. Appoint one person from the team to collate the answers.

Ideally, at this point, if the parish priest has not been able to join you, then ask him to join you at another meeting so that the group can discuss their findings with him. Again, this should be a positive exercise with an eye to the future, not a glass half-empty session.

Parish audit

A parish audit in the light of *Evangelii Nuntiandi* and *Evangelii Gaudium*

Some questions for you to consider in assessing how welcoming your parish is to others

The purpose of this evaluation is two-fold. Firstly, it should be used before the Parish Evangelisation Team begins planning its actions. You are looking to **identify** what evangelisation programmes already exist: of these, which ones are doing well? Which need more attention? The team can then determine whether to focus their efforts on existing evangelisation efforts or initiate new ones.

This assessment tool may be used throughout the evangelisation process to determine progress and obtain new ideas. As the group develops its plan for evangelisation, it is important to keep the needs and diversity of parishioners in mind: by way of a prompt you will find a list of the diverse grouping that you may encounter in your parish in Formation Meeting 2 (in Chapter Three), where you have already considered the diversity of your parish. Take a few minutes to review the list and identify which of the groups you have in your parish and how you feel their particular needs, in relation to their faith life, are met by your parish.

First impressions

At this point it is useful for you to ask the question: "What is the 'first impression' that strangers get of the parish?" Someone once said: "You only get one chance to make a first impression." This is quite right. In Formation Meeting 1, you looked at first impressions, so review what you discussed during your first meeting. It will be good to once again spend some time assessing the impression that strangers get when entering the parish site. You might see things in a new light now that you have completed your time of formation.

The welcome

The welcome the parish gives is one of the most important tools for evangelisation and can be the cause not only of losing existing parishioners but turning new ones away. Here is a helpful check list for you to reflect upon:

- How are people greeted when they arrive at church?
- Does anyone give out hymn books, Mass books, service sheets, newsletters?
- Do members of the congregation openly greet or welcome others around them?
- Do parishioners greet and welcome people at baptism, funerals and other services?
- Are newcomers formally welcomed at the start of a service?

- Do you have some form of Mass booklet that indicates to a non-Catholic visitor where to stand or sit during the Mass/service?
- Are people who cannot receive Communion invited to come forward for a blessing?
- Does the priest or designated lay person greet people at the back of church?

How child friendly is your church?

How many times have we seen parents with small children rush out because they are embarrassed by a noisy offspring who is just bored, and Mum or Dad feel they have become the subject of the "tut-tut brigade"? Children are the future of the Church, but it is the opinion of the parents that you need to encourage. If they feel that their children are welcome in church, then they too will feel welcome. Again here is a list to aid your assessment of the parish facilities.

- Is there an area where children/toddlers can go without disturbing others?
- Do you provide feeding and changing facilities for babies and young children?
- Is there a Liturgy of the Word for children available?
- Are members of the congregation involved in the children's liturgy?
- Are the children involved in the procession of the gifts?
- Are young children encouraged to come for a blessing at Communion?

- Do young people generally play an active part in the service?

Following up the welcome, here are a few ideas you may already have in your parish, but if not, you may wish to consider them

- Do you provide tea/coffee after services? Are newcomers openly invited?
- Are there welcome cards for newcomers to fill in to give their name and address?
- Does the parish have a welcome pack to give or send them?
- How soon are newcomers contacted after their first introduction?
- Does your parish have a process for welcoming "returning" Catholics?
- Does the parish organise events specifically to welcome people?

Catering for everyone's needs

- Do you have parking facilities for the disabled? How easy is it for disabled people to access the church?
- Are people with disabilities invited to undertake liturgical ministries?
- Are all social/ethnic groups included in the life of the parish?
- Does the church have a bookstall or repository or library?
- Are there regular social events in the parish?

A parish audit in the light of *Laudato Si'*

After focusing on *Laudato Si'* for two of your formation meetings, take a look at some of the points below, to see if there is anything you could adopt in the parish or encourage parishioners to adopt some of the ideas at home.

Taking action in the parish

Here are a few ideas based on Pope Francis' suggestions in *Laudato Si'* (LS 211):

- Has your parish ever done an energy audit, identifying where consumption could be cut?
- Has your parish considered gradually changing light bulbs to more energy efficient ones as well as perhaps fitting motion sensors in areas where lights tend to be left on for a long time when there is no one in the area?
- Does your parish encourage recycling?
- Does your parish demonstrate care for creation in everything it does?
- Does your parish use disposable cups and plates, instead of washable ones? Replacing the disposable ones is more environmentally friendly
- Does your parish property have trees on it? If not and there is room, consider planting some
- Do we ensure that learning about the importance of care for God's creation is a part of parish life?
- Does your parish actively support the two CAFOD Fast Days in the year (spring and autumn)?

- Does the parish use the resources provided by CAFOD at the time of the Fast Days to help educate people about poverty and the developing world?
- Does your parish have a regular opportunity for parishioners to bring foodstuff, clothing, bedding, toiletries and similar items for the homeless and those who are reliant on food parcels? Does your parish have links with one or two local centres that feed the homeless or have a food bank?
- Does your parish have a local secretary/promoter for the Association for the Propagation of the Faith (APF Missio), promoting the famous "Red Boxes" from APF, which help missionary outreach throughout the world in the developing nations?

"Evangelising is in fact the grace and vocation proper to the Church, her deepest identity"

– Pope Paul VI, Evangelii Nuntiandi

A parish audit in the light of *Amoris Laetitia*

In the light of your two formation meetings based on *Amoris Laetitia*, here are some questions for you to consider with regard to how your parish supports families. It is not expected that every parish should offer all that is listed. The important point is that we create a parish community where families feel that they belong, whether they are passing through or staying for many years. People want their parishes to actively support parents/carers/families. Are they given space to develop as Christians themselves, and how much help do they get as they introduce their faith to their children? Does your parish community help families of all dimensions to feel comfortable and valued?

Some points and questions to consider

- Do you provide baptism preparation? Do non-Catholic partners feel welcome?
- Do you offer practical support to young families, for example, a clothes exchange, second-hand baby equipment service, toy library and other things helpful to young families?
- Do you have a parent and toddler group open to all families connected to the parish and in the neighbourhood?
- Do you offer support for children who do not attend Catholic schools?
- How do you cater for non-Catholic partners when children are preparing for the sacraments?

- Is your sacramental preparation programme sensitive to families in different domestic situations? Or does it assume that all children are living with two parents in a traditional family setting?
- Does everybody know who is responsible in the parish for the safeguarding of children and vulnerable adults?
- What is available for young people in your parish?
- How does your parish link in with young people at secondary school?
- Do young people in your parish participate in any deanery/diocesan activity, for example, Lourdes pilgrimages, pilgrimage groups, World Youth Day events?
- Do you have any church services specifically for, or focused on, young people?
- How do you help and support parents of young children and teenagers?
- Do you run any courses or groups for single, separated or divorced parents?
- Do you have any parish activities where all the family can join in and have fun such as socials, outings, sports events, weekend breaks?
- Does your liturgy (words and music) reflect your community? Can parishioners participate actively in the celebration?
- Do you have a parish magazine? Is it sent to housebound/elderly parishioners?
- Do you provide opportunities for sharing skills, experiences and information?
- Do you have a supply of information leaflets available about life's problem areas?

- Do you know where to find help for families who are looking for support with social issues/problems such as bullying, drugs/alcohol abuse, domestic violence?
- If you have a parish primary school, do you liaise with the head teacher in order to find out if there are families who would benefit from discreet help and support from the local community?
- As time goes on, in our parishes we will find ourselves being the recipients of more and more families who are displaced, refugees and migrants, who have no family of their own to support them – how can we befriend them and help them?
- In a given academic year there may be a family in your school who experiences the tragic loss of one of the parents or even a child. Again, how are we to support them as a parish and not just as a school community?
- Do we ensure that families who have children with special needs know that they are all welcome in the parish?
- Do we know the people in our parishes well enough to be able to celebrate milestones in marriage and family life publicly with the whole community?
- When couples are celebrating a silver wedding, ruby or golden wedding anniversary do we mark that occasion with the parish community?
- Would couples feel comfortable in asking the priest to incorporate a renewal of their marriage vows or a special blessing at their regular Sunday Mass in front of the whole community?

- Do we encourage members of the parish to attend the weddings celebrated in our church?
- What are we doing/could we be doing to support and welcome those who are separated, divorced/re-married, so that they can play as full a part as possible in the life of the community?

And finally

Consider how we can allow the Holy Spirit to move us towards innovative, creative solutions that care for people and God's creation.

After giving consideration to the results of your survey, it is now time to look at an action plan. The following will assist you in the way forward.

This action plan can help a parish to move forward in welcoming and helping to engage new and returning Catholics.

Action plan/Next steps

ACTION PLAN

Parish Name: ....

Key aspects of our Parish Welcome that we want to share and celebrate are:

-
-
-
-
-

Short-term actions that we are going to take to develop the ministry of Welcome in our Parish are:

-
-
-
-
-

Obstacles/barriers we have identified in developing our Parish Welcome are:

-
-
-
-
-

A few considerations in your Action Plan:

The Parish will provide for faith development in the following areas:

- Parish renewal programmes
- Retreats
- Scripture study
- Liturgy of the Word with children
- Youth programmes
- Faith-sharing groups
- Devotional development
- Faith formation
- Marriage and family life.

The Parish sees the Eucharist as central to parish life. We will foster its development in the following ways:

- Greeting and welcome
- Fostering prayer-filled liturgy and active participation
- Ensuring that communal worship is accessible to all
- Providing opportunity for people to meet together after Mass.

How will parishioners be involved in Sacramental celebrations?

-
-
-
-
-
-
-
-

How will your Parish reach out to the wider community?

-
-
-
-
-
-

Training parishioners to listen and offer a sincere welcome to returning Catholics such as:

- Divorced and separated
- Remarried
- Hurting
- Hungry
- Stressed
- Emotionally burdened
- Victims of violence
- Former prisoners
- Lesbian, gay, bisexual, transgender
- Those feeling alone or isolated in the community.

List any other ways in which your Parish can evangelise:

-
-
-
-
-
-
-
-
-

You have taken time to look in detail at your own parish. By now you should have a plan for its future growth. You have taken time and given a great deal of commitment to being formed into a Parish Evangelisation Team. Keeping in mind that the role of the Team is to be the **evangelising conscience of the parish** you are now ready to work alongside your fellow parishioners in doing the Lord's work and proclaiming the Good News of Jesus Christ.

Below is an extract from an address by Pope Francis, which we were privileged to hear at the Conference on the New Evangelisation and *Evangelii Gaudium* in Rome, Thursday 18 September – Saturday 20 September 2014.

Please, let us not run after the voice of the sirens that call to make of pastoral care a convulsed series of initiatives, without succeeding in gathering the essential of the commitment of evangelisation. Sometimes it seems that we are more preoccupied to multiply activities rather than to be attentive to persons and to their encounter with God. Pastoral care that does not have this attention soon becomes sterile. Let us not forget to do as Jesus did with his disciples: after they had gone to the villages to proclaim the Gospel, they returned happy with their successes, but Jesus took them apart, to a solitary place to be awhile together with them (cf. Mark 6:31). Pastoral care without prayer and contemplation will never reach people's hearts. It will stay at the surface without making it possible for the seed of the Word of God to take root, germinate, grow and bear fruit (cf. Matthew 13:1-23). (**Pope Francis, Rome,19 September 2014**)

In the Appendix we have included the full text of this address by Pope Francis, together with a reflection called "A Parable for today's Church" from Donal Harrington and Julie Kavanagh's *Prayers for Parish Groups*. Reflecting on these may help you as a team to understand that Jesus does not ask you to work in the "Vineyard" without giving you the tools to do the work and the courage to sustain you.

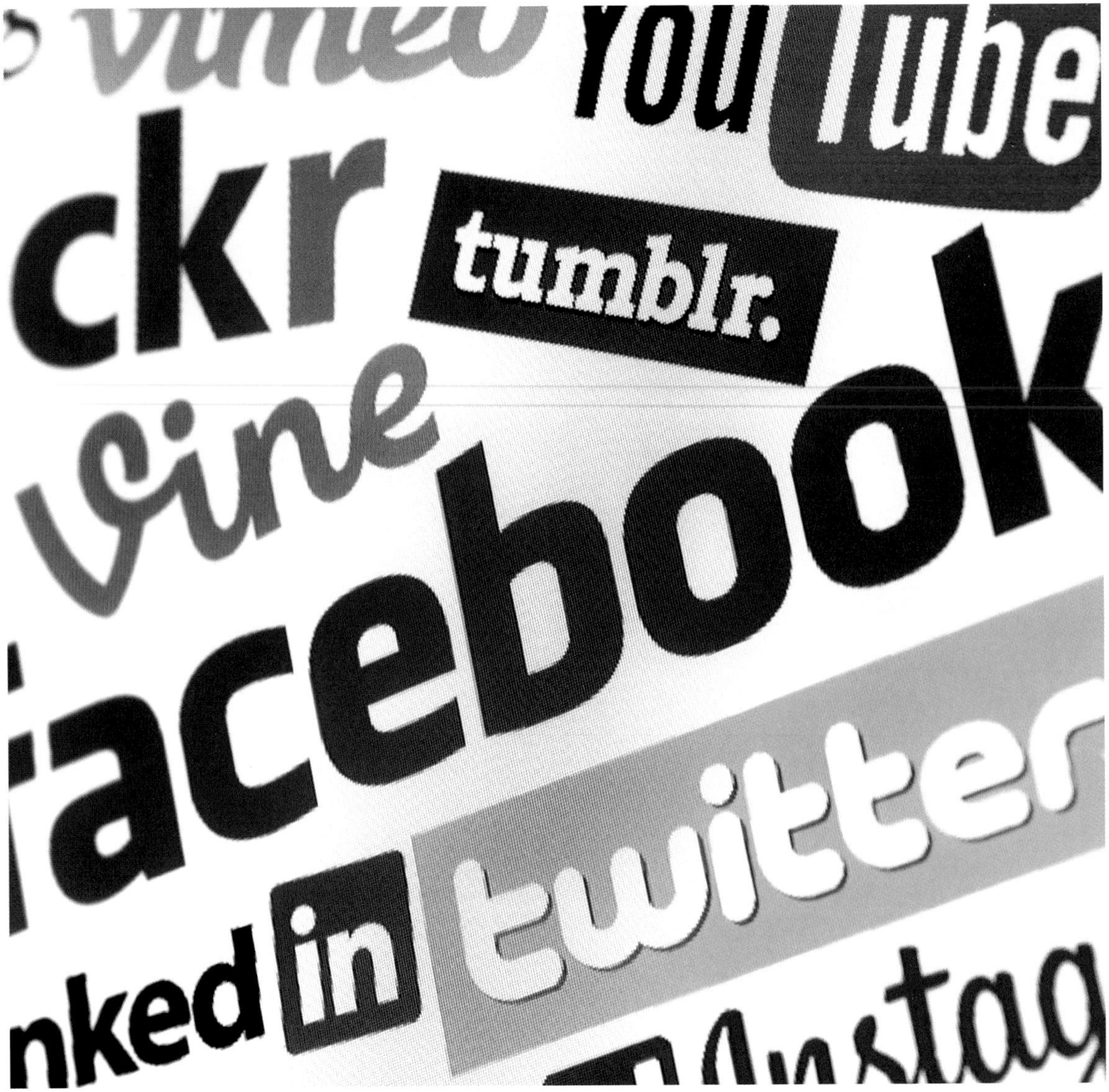
tumblr.
vine

CHAPTER EIGHT
(resources)

The media, social media and the New Evangelisation

"Good communication helps us to grow closer, to know one another better, and ultimately, to grow in unity."
– Pope Francis, Message for the 48th World Communications Day,
1 June 2014

New Evangelisation commentators and authors alike, from popes to religious journalists, constantly remind us that the New Evangelisation is not about a new message. The Good News does not change. The call of the New Evangelisation is about the challenge to find new methods of transmitting the Good News in our current culture and society.

Now that you have completed your time of formation as a Parish Evangelisation Team, you could begin to consider the possibilities presented by the use of the media and the new social media in the work of evangelisation in your parish. Once again, a gentle reminder that the members of the Parish Evangelisation Team don't necessarily have to be the people to move this aspect of evangelisation forward in the parish, but they should be raising the question, "Is there anything that we can do in this area of communication in order to evangelise people?" There will undoubtedly be people in your parish with expertise in this field, maybe even people whose profession is communication, or the use of social media – these are the people we need to engage to help us grow in this area.

At the *Evangelii Gaudium* Conference in the Vatican in September 2014, which we attended, Professor Raphael Chainarong Monthienvichienchai spoke of the dramatic rise in the use of mobile technologies. He cited a United Nations study published in 2013, which certainly made listeners pay attention. It was about mobile phones and toilets. He informed us that the UN report states that out of the world's estimated 7 billion people, more than 6 billion have access to mobile phones, while far fewer, only 4.5 billion people, have access to clean, working toilets.

It was an interesting way to catch our attention. He then went on to speak of the different ways of looking at the use of social media in evangelisation. We can see new media as yet another tool to help us to reach people with the message of the Gospel. By means of the various forms of social media, we can reach out to the peripheries and draw people in, so that they can hear the word of God and understand it better. Another way is to see the digital, online, virtual world itself as a new space which is itself in need of evangelisation.

The incredible advances in communications give us the opportunity to use many new methods of outreach in the service of the Gospel. The widespread availability of internet access prompted Pope Francis to say in his message for the World Communications Day 2014:

The internet, in particular, offers immense possibilities for encounter and solidarity. This is something truly good, a gift from God.

There are some problems, but the drawbacks should not justify our hesitance to embrace the social media. The ability to communicate through new technology is ultimately a vast human achievement, their rapid growth challenges the Church to adopt the best of them in its service of transmitting our faith in the Gospel message.

In this chapter, we will look at some of the new technologies that we could harness in the service of the Gospel and the New Evangelisation.

The internet and parish websites

Twenty years ago, there were approximately two hundred and fifty thousand internet sites. In 2016 there were over a billion of them. Is your parish on the internet?

A website is no longer just a nice thing to have. Today, a presence online has become an essential element of interacting with new people as well as your existing congregation. But parishes need to have a clear vision of why they want to have the presence on the web.

The communications future that we were promised long ago is here right now, and is constantly changing. Are you, as a parish, set up to utilise it?

We've all heard the statistics of how many people own smartphones and iPads and use social networks such as Facebook and Twitter, but do we realise how profoundly these new devices are changing how we communicate? For instance, many more people now check the news multiple times a day, instead of waiting for the evening broadcasts. People use the internet not just for email and searching for information, they use it to pay bills and make contributions, to find out what their relatives across the world, the country or across town are doing, to make dinner reservations, to review films and books, to buy almost anything, and to catch up with the grandchildren.

Three questions we could ask ourselves:
- What does the New Evangelisation look like in this world of communications?
- How can we help build stronger relationships with fellow parishioners (and others)?
- How can we increase the effectiveness of our evangelisation efforts by using the tools of twenty-first-century communications?

We used to ask ourselves, "What do we need to tell people?" Now we also have to ask ourselves, "What do people want to hear from us?"

People no longer wait for the town crier, or the evening news broadcast, or the morning paper, or even the Sunday homily, to come to them.

- When parishioners need **information,** they will seek it and find it
- When they need **guidance,** they will look for it
- When they need **community,** they will connect to it.

But are we able to deliver these things via our parish community and its media outreach? We and they are living in the Digital Continent, as Pope Benedict XVI called it.

The call of the New Evangelisation should be encouraging us to have a renewed focus on resources that offer advice and encouragement for Catholics living their vocations in secular environments.

We have to embrace a culture of innovation and experimentation in communications. This cannot be overemphasised. The new platforms of communications are continually shifting. Who would have imagined just a few years ago that the term "iPad" would have become such a common household term?

Historically, the Church has patiently waited for new technologies to settle in to people's normal rhythms. We do not have that luxury today. The challenges of this moment in communications technology are a boundless opportunity for evangelisation, if we are willing to speak… and listen. The back-and-forth digital communications spreading like wildfire across our dioceses is our chance to bring the Gospel to millions of Catholics. We have to be in the digital conversations. And we have to listen, too.

Just as the Church learned how to use the book and film to proclaim the Good News to the ends of the earth, so today we must teach ourselves to use these new tools to help people find the faith in their ordinary days and in their times of need.

A parish website shows others outside your own local community that you have something to share, and it is good to highlight what your parish feels is unique about it. It has to be said that a parish website is just that: a parish's website and not the parish priest's website!

A parish website can once again be a great way of involving younger parishioners in its building and maintenance. That, in fact, is probably one of the most important things to say about a parish website: it needs to be maintained, kept up-to-date and relevant. The latest parish newsletter should be the current one, not one from three months or three years previously!

The daily Mass schedule for the current week needs to be accessible. Contact information, ministries and groups must be correct and up-to-date.

The parish website is a great tool for indicating the vibrancy of a parish community. People other than your own parishioners will discover your website, in a sense, by accident. Several years ago, someone in Florida, who had emigrated to the States, found our parish website. She was curious to know about the local Catholic Grammar School she had attended. Through the email link on the website we were able to update her on the information she requested, arrange for her to visit the parish and her former school on her next trip to the UK and we forged new and lasting relationships.

A parish website must be both **welcoming** and **inviting**. Encourage people to actually visit the parish if they are in the vicinity. Tell them how to find the church (especially important if you are not on a main road, but in the middle of a housing estate or heavily built-up area), give a contact name and the all-important telephone number and email address.

In devising your website content, it is important that you follow your diocesan safeguarding guidelines, especially in relation to personal telephone numbers and photographs. Never publish photographs that identify one specific person, without their permission. All invitations to contact a particular group or ministry should always be directed through the parish office.

In short, keep your parish website current, informative, attractive and easy to navigate.

A good general rule is that you should need no more than three clicks of the computer mouse to be in the place you want to be on any website. Any more than three clicks and people lose interest, meaning you could lose a valuable opportunity to reach out to someone through your website.

Pope Francis in his 2014 message for the 48th World Communications Day comments that:

By means of the internet, the Christian message can reach "to the ends of the earth" (Acts 1:8). Keeping the doors of our churches open also means keeping them open in the digital environment so that people, whatever their situation in life, can enter, and so that the Gospel can go out to reach everyone.

Some questions that you could ask in relation to your parish's presence on the worldwide web:

- How is your parish website representing the beauty of our Catholic faith?
- Is the homepage inviting and attractive to look at?
- Does it invite the visitor to explore further?
- Is it well written?
- Does the website have all the "basic" information on it, such as Mass times, parish address, phone number, and directions?
- Does your website include inspiring stories about your parishioners?
- Is your parish website mission driven or member driven? Are you using your site to evangelise the seeker and the disengaged?
- Are your parish events featured on your homepage? Do your events answer the Who, What, When, Where, and Why?

Emails

Many people now use emails as their main method of communication, accessing their emails wherever they are via smartphones and tablets. If you have a parish email address, is the inbox regularly checked? If not, it is as useful as an out-of-date website – of no use!

Several years ago, we invited people to sign up to receive the weekly newsletter by email. It is such a simple thing, but it keeps people in touch with the parish community and the latest news and other aspects of what's happening in and around the parish. We have found that former parishioners who have moved away from the area are keen to keep up with what is happening in the parish. We find that, as some of our parishioners find it more difficult to get out each week to Mass, perhaps especially during a harsh winter, they like to receive the newsletter by email. Students who have gone to university keep in touch with us through receiving the newsletter each week by email, and on many occasions, family members of our parishioners, who live away from our area, also receive it.

To set this up was incredibly simple. We created a distribution group in our email address book, adding the addresses of parishioners who wanted to receive the weekly e-newsletter. As soon as the newsletter is completed each week, we create a PDF document, attach it to the distribution group of email addresses, and send it out with one click of the computer mouse. It is all done in about the same amount of time it takes to physically print the first five copies. Over 400 people receive the parish newsletter by email each Saturday.

Twitter

Several years ago, in our own parish we became converts to the world of Twitter. We have been seeing the potential of it for the past few years, and always spotting new opportunities for using it. It was one of our parishioners who got us interested in it by promising to "set it all up for you" and to teach us how to use it. So we entered somewhat nervously into, what was for us, this new world of Twitter, joining the other 320 million users.

We encouraged members of the parish to "follow us" on Twitter, and began "tweeting". At first, only twenty or so people followed us, but then the numbers gradually increased. Currently there are 280 people following the parish Twitter account (which, for an average-sized parish, is a pretty good number).

So what do we use it for? Firstly, from the very outset, it is the parish Twitter account and not the parish priest's! So it refers only to parish events and parish outreach, and doesn't deal with what the parish priest had for lunch!

Here are a few ideas for using Twitter based on our own experience:

Baptisms

Whenever we have baptisms, we tweet a message after the baptism asking people to pray for the newly baptised children (or adults) and their families, expressing our welcome to them as they become members of the Church. Increasingly these tweets are re-tweeted by their families (and then they begin to follow us!).

Weddings

The day before a wedding we tweet asking people to keep the couple in their prayers on their wedding day. Once the wedding service has concluded, we take a photograph of the couple and, with their permission, we tweet the photograph with a message of congratulations, usually before the couple have reached the venue for their reception. Again, these tweets are rapidly re-tweeted or liked by the couple's family and friends. (A "like" is how users of Twitter express their appreciation or agreement with what you have tweeted, or in the case of Facebook what you have posted.)

Funerals

The day before a funeral, and again on the day of a funeral in our parish, we tweet, asking people to remember the deceased and their family in their prayers. Many people, including the bereaved family pick up and re-tweet these prayer requests and so the circle of prayer extends.

Other Sacraments of Initiation

Throughout the year we celebrate the sacramental milestones in the life of our younger parishioners, such as their presentation for the sacraments of confirmation and First Holy Communion, and of course, when the celebrations take place, we again ask on Twitter for people to pray for the group of children.

Parish pilgrimages

By posting photographs and news of what we have done, and where we have visited, we use Twitter to keep in touch with the parish during any parish pilgrimage. Many of our followers reply to us during the pilgrimages and re-tweet our communications. We find also that family members of our pilgrims usually follow the journey on Twitter.

Social events

We have plenty of social events in our parish, providing parishioners with the opportunity to come together and socialise and enjoy each other's company, and so we tweet about these events, including photographs.

We feel that the use of the short messages on Twitter sends out a message of a community that celebrates the welcoming of new members, rejoices with others on the occasion of life-changing events, and also encourages prayers for parishioners and world events.

The beauty of Twitter is that each of our followers has their own followers, so when a tweet is re-tweeted the original message begins to reach even more people.

But it is not only about what we tweet. We also follow others. It is a perfect tool for a speedy check on world events and especially helpful in supplying a short inspirational thought for the daily homily. Most of Pope Francis' morning homilies in the Vatican are tweeted by the time we have our daily Mass!

Despite an initial slight reluctance to use Twitter, we now see it as a tool for the New Evangelisation, which also includes the younger generation in its outreach.

Facebook

A Facebook page brings with it several advantages as another tool in the work of the New Evangelisation. Again there are several questions that you need to ask, such as:

- Why create a Facebook page?
- How do you do it?
- Who will maintain it?
- What do you post to it?

It is important to seek advice from those who understand these things (usually the younger members of our communities) and then enlist their help in setting up and maintaining the page.

A Facebook page provides a parish with several benefits. Firstly, it is an additional avenue to communicate with your parish and beyond. In 2016, Facebook had approximately 1.71 billion monthly active users. Many of these users will be sitting in your pews. Facebook users are typically loyal, checking and updating their page daily.

You will need to decide who will create the page initially and who will be the "Administrators". It is probably a good idea to have a couple of people as Administrators in order to monitor and keep posts and interactions lively. So what do you post on your page? This is the great thing about Facebook. It can be used for a variety of purposes. Here are some ideas:

- Photographs of events
- Announcements of events and links to more information
- Link to a blog post from your clergy and ask a question or initiate a thought. This is a great way to start a conversation
- Videos or articles you find relating to the faith
- Daily readings and reflections.

The parish newsletter

In many ways much of what we have encouraged about the parish website can be said for the weekly newsletter – make it current, informative, attractive, and easy to navigate. Recreate its design at least once a year; move and change items every few weeks; plan content; ensure that there is always something that is going to enrich the reader's faith; help them to reflect on the Sunday scripture readings (they may not remember the wonderfully powerful homily delivered at Mass, but most people will take the newsletter home with them, and read it there that day or during the week – unless of course they have read it during the wonderfully powerful homily itself).

Of course, the extraordinary ministers of the Eucharist who take Communion to the sick and housebound are a very real link with the parish. They should take a newsletter to the sick and housebound people they visit.

The local newspaper and local radio

Are you ever frustrated when it seems that almost everything that happens at a particular church in your area makes it into the local newspaper or on the local radio station, but nothing that your parish organises or does ever appears in this media? Why? Ask yourself the question, "Do we tell them?"

Local newspapers and local radio stations are crying out for local news. This is what sells the papers and maintains audience statistics. Why not ask someone in the parish to be the parish information officer? Their role would be to email the weekly newsletter to the local press and radio station. Follow them on Twitter or Facebook and retweet a good tweet. This draws their attention to the fact that you are a follower. They might then begin following you in the hope of good nuggets of information or a story. Identify someone in your parish who is able to talk to them. Do not be afraid of the media. They can help to share the good news of what we, a vibrant, welcoming and inviting Christian community, are doing in our neighbourhood. The local media needs our "good news stories".

Your local newspaper and radio station can be a great way of spreading the Good News in this time of the New Evangelisation. Many local radio stations have a dedicated faith programme, perhaps each Sunday morning. Our own local radio station has around

40,000 people listening to the Sunday morning Faith programme – if you have the chance to get on there, grab it!

The right use of social media

There are more opportunities than ever before for the Church to share the Good News – are you, as a parish community, making the most of them, even imitating in your own small way the Vatican's use of social media, and heeding the warnings of misuse? Pope Francis in his message for the 50th World Communications Day encourages right use of the internet and social media when he says:

Emails, text messages, social networks and chats can also be fully human forms of communication. It is not technology which determines whether or not communication is authentic, but rather the human heart and our capacity to use wisely the means at our disposal. Social networks can facilitate relationships and promote the good of society, but they can also lead to further polarisation and division between individuals and groups. The digital world is a public square, a meeting-place where we can either encourage or demean one another, engage in a meaningful discussion or unfair attacks. I pray that this Jubilee Year, lived in mercy, "may open us to even more fervent dialogue so that we might know and understand one another better; and that it may eliminate every form of closed-mindedness and disrespect, and drive out every form of violence and discrimination" (*Misericordiae Vultus*, 23). The internet can help us to be better citizens. Access to digital networks entails a responsibility for our neighbour whom we do not see but who is nonetheless real and has a dignity which must be respected. The internet can be used wisely to build a society which is healthy and open to sharing. Communication, wherever and however it takes place, has opened up broader horizons for many people. This is a gift of God which involves a great responsibility. (**Message of His Holiness Pope Francis for the 50th World Communications Day: "Communication and Mercy: A Fruitful Encounter", 24 January 2016**)

And again a couple of years earlier in 2014 he said:

The Church needs to be concerned for, and present in, the world of communication, in order to dialogue with people today and to help them encounter Christ. She needs to be a Church at the side of others, capable of accompanying everyone along the way. The revolution taking place in communications media and in information technologies represents a great and thrilling challenge; may we respond to that challenge with fresh energy and imagination as we seek to share with others the beauty of God. (**Message of His Holiness Pope Francis for the 48th World Communications Day 2014: "Communication at the Service of an Authentic Culture of Encounter", 1 June 2014**)

CHAPTER NINE

Evangelisation through prayer

"Let us try asking ourselves: am I open to the action of the Holy Spirit? Do I pray him to give me illumination, to make me more sensitive to God's things? This is a prayer we must pray every day: 'Holy Spirit, make my heart open to the word of God, make my heart open to goodness, make my heart open to the beauty of God every day.'"

– Pope Francis, General Audience, 15 May 2013

Growing up in the Catholic Church, prayer has always been the centre of life and of course the great prayer of the Church, the Eucharist, is the core of everything we do. Who amongst us has not been given, at some time, a small book of Catholic prayers? And of course we knew that whatever situation arose in our lives, there would be a prayer in there for us to say. So it goes without saying that in order to spread the Good News of Jesus Christ, prayer must be the basis of everything we do.

The New Evangelisation calls us to have confidence in the Gospel, helping us to deepen our love for our faith and to have the confidence to share it with others. It is often not easy to share our love for Jesus Christ and the Church with others and to help others to develop a personal relationship with him, but it is in prayer that our relationship with God is strengthened, nourished and sustained.

Here are some quotes on prayer to reflect on:
For me, prayer is a surge of the heart; it is a simple look turned toward heaven, it is a cry of recognition and of love, embracing both trial and joy. **(St Thérèse of Lisieux)**

Prayer is a vital and personal relationship with the living and true God. **(Catechism of the Catholic Church, 2558)**

Prayer is the living relationship of the children of God with their Father who is good beyond measure, with his Son Jesus Christ and with the Holy Spirit... Thus, the life of prayer is the habit of being in the presence of the thrice-holy God and in communion with him. **(Catechism of the Catholic Church, 2565)**

These quotations describe an encounter or relationship with the Lord. As a Parish Evangelisation Team this is what you seek in prayer. In other words, it is not about "saying our prayers" but encountering

God and focusing on the job at hand. This is the kind of prayer that takes us from knowing on an intellectual level that God loves us to experiencing his love first hand. In other words, we receive love and then we love in return. This is the "surge of the heart" that St Thérèse describes. This kind of prayer makes it possible to encounter God on a daily basis. It builds our intimacy with God and our understanding of his love for us, and that enables us to share his love with others. For you, as a Parish Evangelisation Team whenever you meet, it will be by reflecting on the words of Jesus before and after meetings that you will be reminded that you are there to do God's will in the parish and not your own will.

During the years we have been involved in the work of evangelisation we have encountered many people in many parish situations who have given their lives in proclaiming the word of the Lord. However, in May 2016 we were to experience something quite special, something that would confirm our belief that the fundamental work of evangelisation can only be achieved through prayer and outreach. We were fortunate to be able to join a small group of parishioners and their parish priest, Fr Victor, from Holy Innocents' parish, Orpington, in attending the 27th International Parish Evangelisation Cells Seminar at St Eustorgio in Milan. We must say their enthusiasm was infectious and their commitment and this prayerful evangelisation concept was inspirational. At the seminar there were representatives from twenty-five different countries and from all walks of life.

In May 2009, the Pontifical Council for the Laity gave recognition to this association of lay faithful, issuing a formal recognition of the parish-based evangelisation process of Parish Evangelisation Cells. In September 2015, Pope Francis addressed members at a conference in the Paul VI Audience Hall, Vatican City. The following is an extract from his address:

With your daily commitment, and in communion with the other ecclesial realities, you help the parish community to become a family in which the rich and complex reality of the Church is found (cf *Lumen Gentium*, 8). Meeting in homes to share the joys and expectations that are present in the heart of each person is a genuine experience of evangelisation which closely resembles what took place in the early times of the Church. St Luke recalls it in the Acts of the Apostles, when he suggests that "day by day, attending the temple together and breaking bread in their homes, they partook of food with glad and generous hearts, praising God and having favour with all the people" (2:46-47). You, Cells, strive to make your own this community lifestyle, the ability to welcome everyone while judging no one (cf. *Evangelii Gaudium*, 165). Our judge is the Lord, and if you have in your mouth a judgmental word about someone or another, close your mouth. The Lord gave us this advice: "Judge not, and you will not be judged". Live with people with simplicity, welcome everyone. Why welcome everyone? To offer the experience of God's presence and the love of one's brothers and sisters. Evangelisation senses the strong need of welcome, of closeness, because it is one of the first signs of the communion to which we are called to testify in order to have encountered Christ in our life.

> Parish Evangelisation Cells are not a new concept, but they can return us to a time when people worshipped in their own homes and through prayer and outreach the Church grew and flourished.

To say that the history of Evangelisation Cells is unusual is an understatement. In 1981, Fr Michael Eivers, an American priest, travelled to Seoul, South Korea, to study the evangelisation practices of the largest congregation in the world: David Cho's Yoido Full Gospel Church. Yoido Full Gospel Church is a Pentecostal congregation with approximately 830,000 members divided into thousands of small "cells" for formation, pastoral care and evangelisation. Fr Eivers adapted the Cell idea for a Catholic context and implemented it in his parish in Pembroke Pines, Florida, which grew in membership tremendously as a result.

In 1986 the concept of Cells began to spread around Europe and elsewhere including France, Belgium, Ireland, Italy, Brazil, Venezuela, Eastern Europe and other parts of the world. There are now about 4,300 Evangelisation Cells in Catholic parishes on five continents.

The Cells are made up of lay people who meet weekly or bi-weekly and invite friends to join them. As the Cells grow, other Cells are formed. During the prayer sessions they listen to an audio recording of a formation talk by the parish priest, and share fellowship and prayer. Don Pigi Perini, who brought the concept to the parish of St Eustorgio in Milan, has been organising annual International Parish Evangelisation Cell seminars for many years. The purpose of the International Seminar is to prepare pastoral leaders to use the Cell system in their communities and, although now retired, Don Pigi still takes an active role in the work and formation of the laity involved in the Cells.

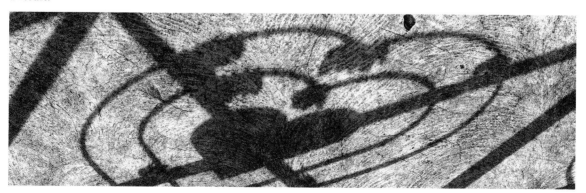

In *The Shape of the Church to Come* (New York, Seabury, 1974), the twentieth-century theologian Karl Rahner said: "The Church of the future will be one built from below by basic communities." From what we could see during our time in Milan, what the Cells are achieving and will continue to achieve is a foundation of prayer-based evangelisation, which complements the practical work of evangelisation that Parish Evangelisation Teams do. We feel privileged to have spent our time at St Eustorgio's and would recommend this concept as a powerful evangelisation tool which embraces prayer as its focus.

Someone who most certainly used prayer as a tool for evangelisation was Brother Nicholas Hutchinson, a De La Salle Brother and a very dear friend of ours. After a lengthy illness, Brother Nick sadly passed away in 2016. Our lasting memory of Nick would be his strength and humility in a time of illness and pain. In his last years, Nick, already a prolific writer, embarked on a new book, *Praying in Serious Illness* (Chelmsford: Matthew James Publishing, 2012). He said he would not live long enough to see it published. However, *Praying in Serious Illness* was published in 2012, four years before his death. During his long illness we received many Christmas cards in which he apologised for still being alive! Perhaps his greatest gift in this very difficult time was that he was able to help other people in similar circumstances to pray. For many people Nick was a source of comfort and strength, and with his help and through his many books, everyone who contacted him was able to find some comfort in prayer, and in return he drew comfort from them. He prayed constantly for strength and also for all those who touched his life and made his last years more meaningful for everyone.

Nick showed us that it is through prayer that we are able to help people renew their relationship with God and it is through prayer and outreach that we can rebuild the Kingdom that is our legacy in Christ.

The following prayer is taken from *Lord, Teach Us to Pray* by Br Nicholas Hutchinson FSC (1954–2016):

> Lord Jesus,
>   I ask you to open my eyes
>   as you did with the blind man,
>   so that I may really see.
>
> Tune my ears
>   as you did
>   with the man who was deaf and dumb,
>   so that I may really hear
>   what you are saying to me.
>   May the many experiences of my senses
>   remind me to be aware of others
>   and of all that is around me.
>
> May all that I experience
>   lead me closer to you.
> Amen.

(reference: Nicholas Hutchinson, *Lord, Teach Us to Pray* (Chelmsford: Matthew James Publishing, 1999), and also as prayer 22 "Open my eyes and ears" <http://www.prayingeachday.org/100prayers.pdf>, accessed 20 Jan. 2017)

CONCLUSION

"Loving others is a spiritual force drawing us to union with God; indeed, one who does not love others 'walks in the darkness' (1 John 2:11), 'remains in death' (1 John 3:14) and 'does not know God' (1 John 4:8)."

– Pope Francis, Evangelii Gaudium, 272

"Love alone is the answer to that yearning for infinite happiness."

– Pope Francis, Message for Lent 2016

Jesus came so that all people may have life and have it to the full. As Christians we believe that we have that life, and therefore we must imitate Jesus in wanting to share the fullness of life with all those we encounter.

In the chapters of our book we have tried to provide the structure and the means for parish priest and lay people to develop a programme of formation for Parish Evangelisation Teams. We have also tried to look at the work of these teams in different aspects of the life of the Church, and we hope that by taking the four papal documents as our foundation we have been able to help teams form a more focused understanding of the challenges that the recent popes and current Pope are offering us as Church. We hope that the ideas and materials that we have shared with you will be of use in moving your team forward and providing you with the means to guide your parish to a more meaningful encounter with Jesus.

In the course of your work you will meet many people who have concerns about the lack of people, old and young, in our parishes. We have to reach out to all age groups, and invite them to come and see what we have discovered as the expression of the fullness of life in Jesus Christ. If you approach each and every group in your parish, in whatever situation you encounter them, you must see it as an opportunity to evangelise. You will soon realise that it is in the ordinariness of life that we find Jesus. People like the familiar – they want to shop near to where they live, they want to meet their friends in the community in which they live. So the Church must be a vibrant and inviting "meeting place" for them where they can experience the closeness and support of a parish community.

Once people have experienced an invitation and a welcome, they may change their impression of the "stodgy church institution" that so many people seem to have. It's the experience of community that will keep them coming back, hopefully, week after week. People will generally take on responsibility in their parish community when they realise that they are needed, and that they have something to offer, their gifts and talents, that they can use for the good of, and at the service of, their local church community.

We will never be done with the work of evangelisation. There will also be people to reach out to, people to share the Good News with, and people to help experience the fullness of life offered by Jesus Christ.

(reference: Paul Cannon & Sharon Beech, *Welcome to Witness* (Chawton: Redemptorist Publications, 2014), 83-84)

If we are to be evangelisers we must embrace the work of evangelisation and take on the task of walking with people towards a closer encounter with Jesus. Just as the Lord walked with his disciples and they listened to his teaching, we too must walk with our fellow human beings and share our understanding of the message Jesus brings.

If you embarked upon the journey of formation as a member of a Parish Evangelisation Team, we hope that we have given you a larger appetite to look deeper into the ways in which we can evangelise, and it's only now that the real journey begins.

And so our concluding thought would be the following reflection from St Teresa of Avila:

Christ has no body but yours,
No hands, no feet on earth but yours,
Yours are the eyes with which he looks compassion
  on this world,
Yours are the feet with which he walks to do good,
Yours are the hands, with which he blesses all the
  world.
Yours are the hands, yours are the feet,
Yours are the eyes, you are his body.

APPENDIX

Pope Francis' address to the Conference on the New Evangelisation and *Evangelii Gaudium* (Friday 19 September 2014)

Dear Brothers and Sisters, Good afternoon,

I am pleased to take part in your work and I thank Archbishop Rino Fisichella for his introduction. I am also grateful for this setting of "life": this is life! Thank you.

You work in the pastoral care of diverse Churches in the world, and you are meeting to reflect together on the pastoral project of the *Evangelii Gaudium*. In fact, I myself wrote that this document has a "programmatic significance and important consequences" (paragraph 25). And it cannot be otherwise when dealing with the principal mission of the Church, that is, evangelisation! There are times, however, in which this mission becomes more urgent and our sense of responsibility needs to be rekindled.

What comes to mind, first of all, are the words of the Gospel according to Matthew, where it is said that when Jesus "saw the crowds, he had compassion for them, because they were harassed and helpless, like sheep without a shepherd" (9:36). How many people, in the existential peripheries of our time, are "tired and exhausted" and await the Church, they are waiting for us! How can they be reached? How can the experience of faith, the love of God, the encounter with Jesus be shared with them? This is the responsibility of our communities and of our pastoral care.

The Pope does not have the task of offering "a detailed and complete analysis of contemporary reality" (*Evangelii Gaudium*, 51), but to invite all the Church to scrutinise the signs of the times that the Lord offers us unceasingly. So many signs are present in our communities, and the Lord places so many opportunities before us in order to recognise his presence in the world today! Amid negative situations, which as always, make more noise, we also see many signs which instill hope and give courage. These signs, as *Gaudium et Spes* states, must be scrutinised in the light of the Gospel (cf. nn 4, 44 [chapter 4 paragraph 44]): this is the "acceptable time" (cf. 2 Corinthians 6:2), it is the moment of firm commitment, it is the context in which we are called to labour in order to cultivate the Kingdom of God (cf. John 4:35-36). Unfortunately, we see so much poverty and loneliness in today's world! So many people live in great suffering and ask the Church to be a sign of the closeness, of the goodness, of the solidarity and of the mercy of the Lord. This is a task which pertains in a special way to all those who have the responsibility of pastoral care: from the bishop in his diocese to the priest in his parish, from the deacons in service to charity to the men and women catechists in their ministry of spreading the faith.... Clearly, all those occupied in the various spheres of pastoral care are called to recognise and interpret these signs of the times in order to provide a wise and generous response. In the face of so many pastoral exigencies, before the people's many requests, we run the risk of becoming frightened and withdrawing into ourselves in a fearful and defensive attitude. And this gives rise to the temptation of self-sufficiency and of clericalism, that codification of the faith in rules and regulations, as the scribes, the Pharisees, the doctors of the law did in the time of Jesus. To us, everything will be clear and set in order, but the faithful and those in search will still hunger and thirst for God. I have also said several times that the Church seems to me to be a field hospital: so many wounded people who ask us for closeness, who ask us for what they asked of Jesus: closeness, warmth. And with this attitude of the scribes, of the doctors of the law and of the Pharisees, we will never give a witness of closeness.

There is a second word which causes me to reflect. When Jesus tells the episode of the vineyard owner who, in need of workers, left the house at various times of the day to call labourers to come to his vineyard (cf. Matthew 20:1-16). He did not go out only once. In the parable, Jesus says that he went out at least five times: at dawn, at 9:00, at midday, at 3:00 and 5:00 in the afternoon – maybe he will still come to us! There was much work to do in the vineyard and this landlord spent almost all his time going down the streets and to the town squares to seek workers. Think of those of the last hour: no one had called them; who knows how they must have felt, because at the end of the day they would have brought nothing home to feed their children. Thus, all those in charge of pastoral care can take this parable as a good example. To go out at various times of day to go and meet the many who are in search of the Lord. To reach the weakest and the poorest in order to give them the support of feeling useful in the Lord's vineyard, were it even for only an hour.

Another aspect: please, let us not pursue the voice of the sirens who call us to perform pastoral care in a disjointed series of initiatives, without managing to grasp the essential commitment of evangelisation. At times it seems that we are more concerned with redoubling activities than with being attentive to the people and their encounter with God. Pastoral care which does not pay attention to this becomes, little by little, sterile. Let us not forget to do as Jesus did with his disciples: after they had gone into the villages

> *"Blessed are those who endure in peace, for by You, Most High, they shall be crowned"*
> – St Francis of Assisi, Canticle of Brother Sun and Sister

to spread the message of the Gospel, they returned happy about their success; but Jesus took them aside, to a lonely place to stay with them for a while (cf. Mark 6:31). Pastoral care without prayer and contemplation can never reach the heart of the people. It will stop at the surface without allowing the Word of God to take root, to sprout, to grow and bear fruit (cf. Matthew 13:1-23).

I know that all of you work hard, and for this I want to leave you with a last important word: patience. Patience and perseverance. The Word of God entered with "patience" at the moment of the Incarnation, and was constant until death on the Cross. Patience and perseverance. We do not have a "magic wand" for everything, but we trust in the Lord who accompanies us and who never abandons us. In the difficulties as in disappointments which are present, not infrequently, in our pastoral work, we must never fail to have faith in the Lord and in prayer which sustains us. In any case, let us not forget that help is given to us, in the first place, precisely by the many whom we have drawn close to and supported. Let us do good, but without expecting a reward. Let us sow and bear witness. Testimony is the beginning of an evangelisation which touches the heart and transforms it. Words without testimony do not work, they are useless! Testimony is what brings and validates the word.

Thank you for your commitment! I bless you and, please, do not forget to pray for me, because I must speak often and bear a bit of the Christian witness! Thank you.

Let us pray to Our Lady, the Mother of Evangelisation: Hail, Mary, full of grace, the Lord is with thee: blessed art thou among women, and blessed is the fruit of thy womb, Jesus. Holy Mary, Mother of God, pray for us sinners, now, and at the hour of our death. Amen.

A Parable for today's Church

It was time for the travellers to move out from the safety of the hut. The hut they were in was familiar and well-lit, but they knew that it could no longer serve them. It was time to venture out into dark and unfamiliar terrain, to seek out a place of life. As they moved away from the hut, the light its windows cast on the world outside grew dim, until there was very little to guide them. They had to move along tentatively. The directions they decided on were often mistaken and they had to rely on each other for any progress they made.

Not all shared the same feelings about what they were undertaking. Where one grew frustrated, another continued to trust. Where one took heart from the adventure, another started to turn back to the light of the hut. It was a strange and unprecedented situation for them all. The only ones who knew where they were going were the ones who turned back, for they were turning to light and familiarity. But anyone embracing the future was at a loss. The only knowledge they possessed was the wisdom that accumulated as they explored their way forward.

This parable speaks to today's church. A time of safety and certainty has come to an end. A routine and predictable way of doing things has ceased to be serviceable. We are in a new situation and do not know what to do, because we have not had such an experience before. We are all at a loss. The only ones who know where they are going are the ones reaching back into the past. Those who look to the future, who wish to explore, must trust instead that moving on out in the power of the Spirit will yield its own wisdom. At first the wisdom will be very little and a bit all over the place, but slowly it will form sure patterns. But there is no way to prove this to those who stand hesitating in the doorway of the hut.

(reference: Donal Harrington and Julie Kavanagh, *Prayer for Parish Groups*, (Dublin: Columba Press, 1998), 154-155)

Further resources

Suggested programmes

Three programmes from the Paulist Evangelization Ministries (Washington DC):

The Journey is a three-part programme of six sessions each. The programme is designed to encourage Catholics and those looking at faith to deepen or discover their personal relationship with Christ. Each meeting uses scripture, DVD footage, prayer and reflection along with small group discussion.

Awakening Faith – Reconnecting with Your Catholic Faith is a six-session programme that helps inactive Catholics return to the Church. A parish can offer *Awakening Faith* any time of the year and repeat it year after year.

Seeking Christ is an eight-session programme aimed at providing a resource for parishes, to welcome and engage people who come enquiring about the Catholic faith. Each session involves a short DVD reflection, scripture passage and take-home sheet. This programme can form the initial enquiry part of an RCIA programme.

Full details of these programmes, and others from Paulist Evangelization Ministries, can be found on their website: <http://www.pemdc.org>